THIS BOOK BELONGS TO THE FOLLOWING:

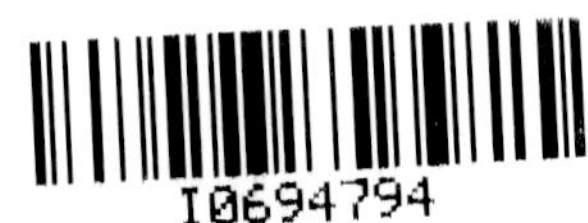

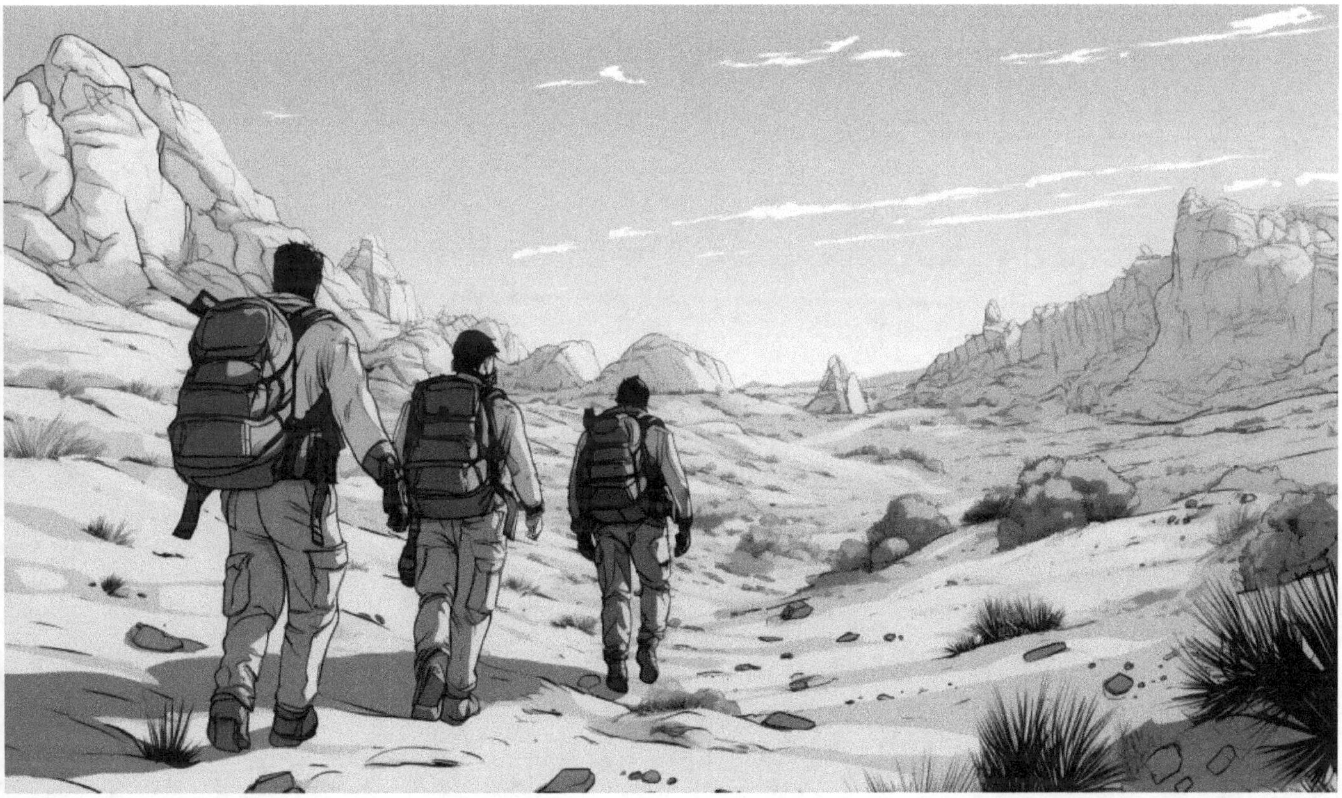

DEDICATED TO THE SERVICE OF THE SAR VOLUNTEERS WHO GIVE THEIR OWN TIME TO BRING THE MISSING HOME!

IMAGES & BOOK CONTENT PROPERTY OF MOJAVE TRADING POST

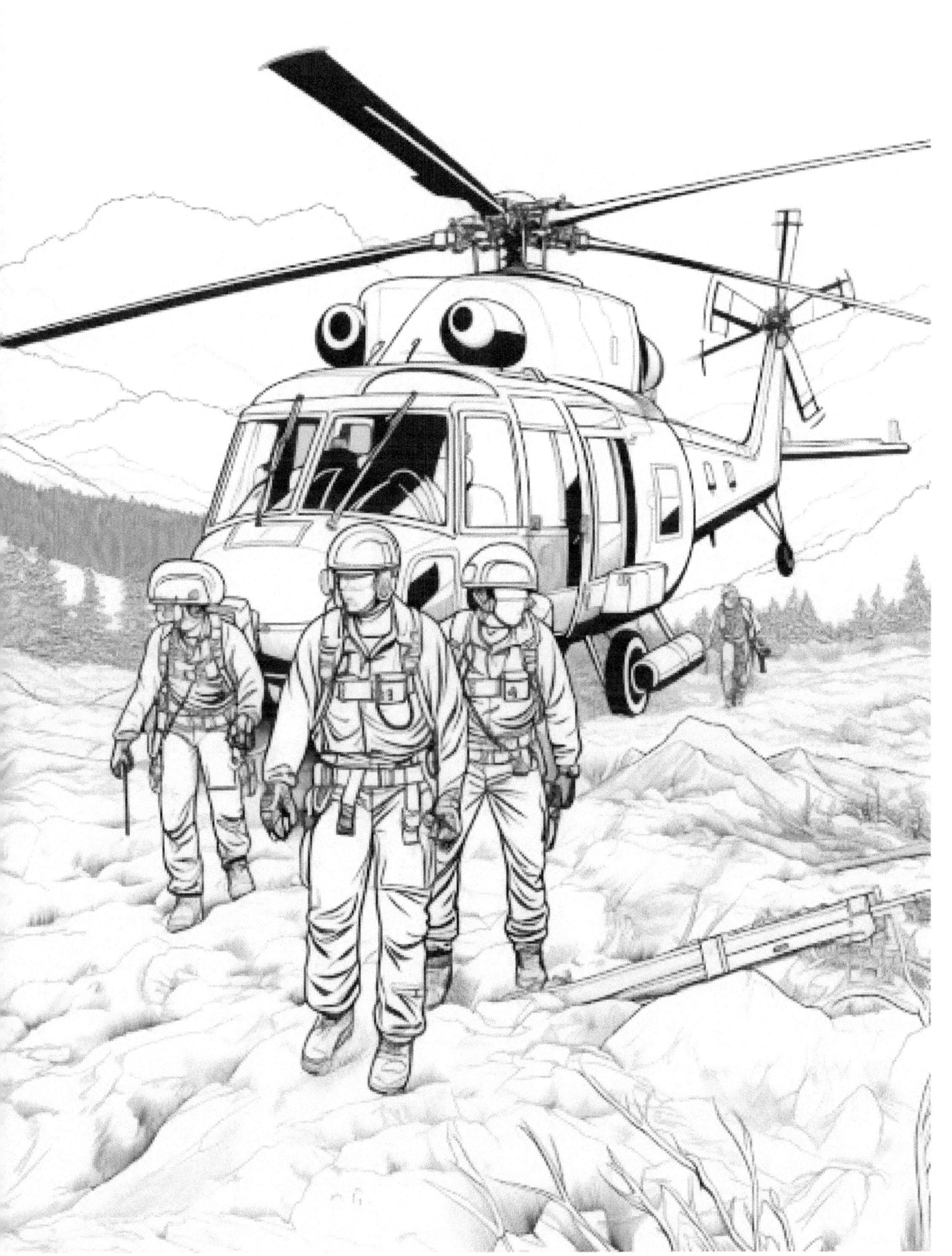

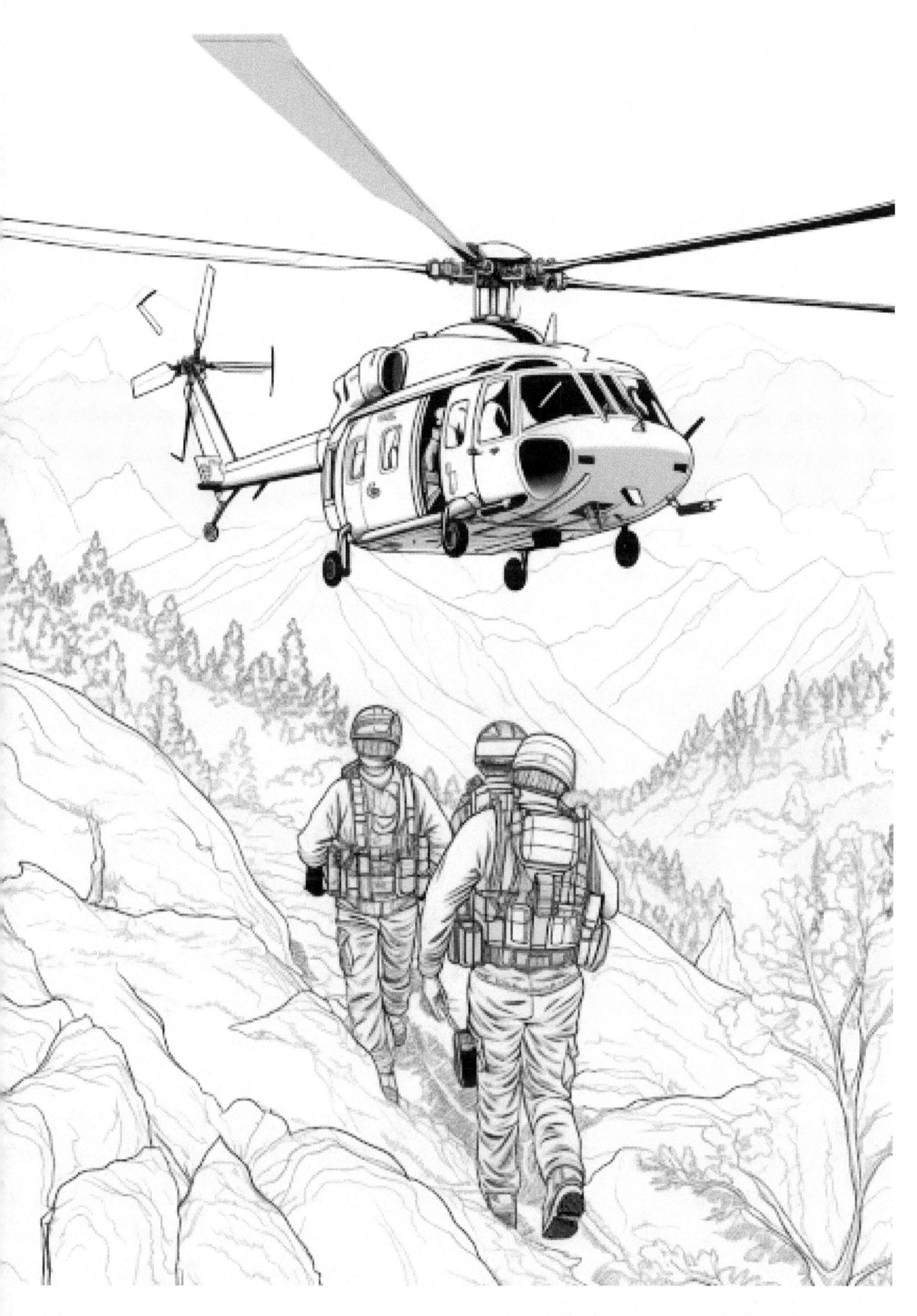

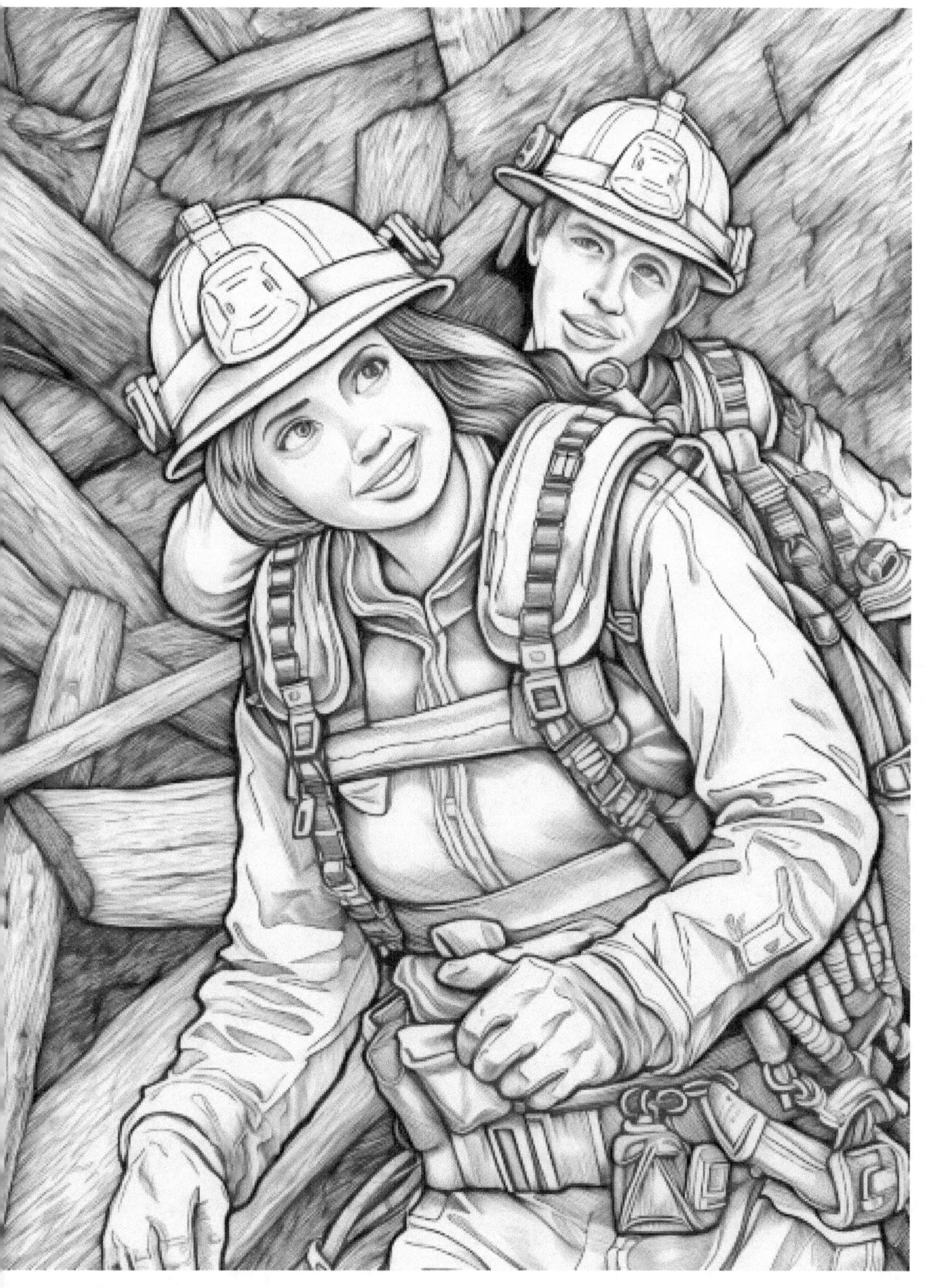

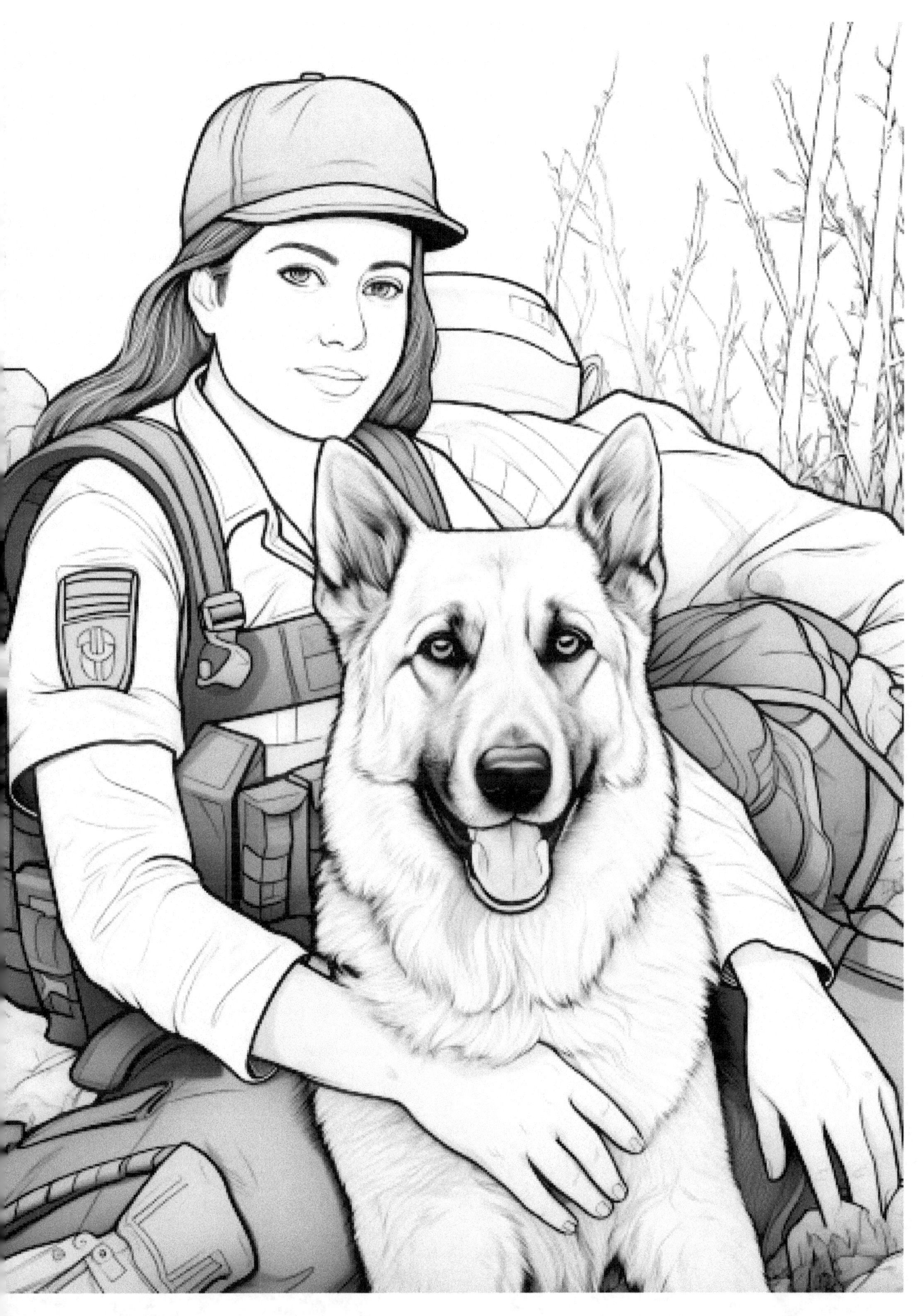

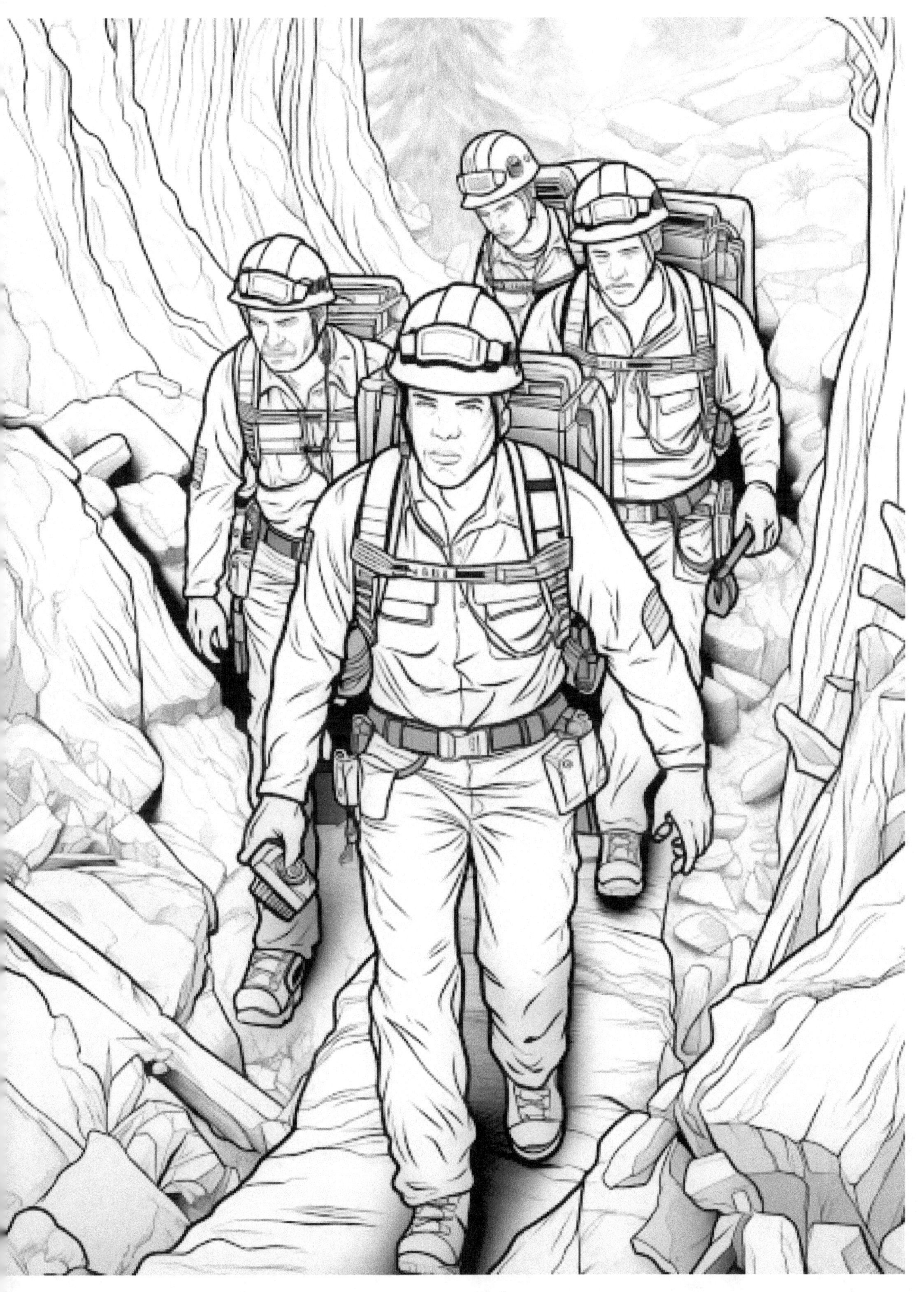

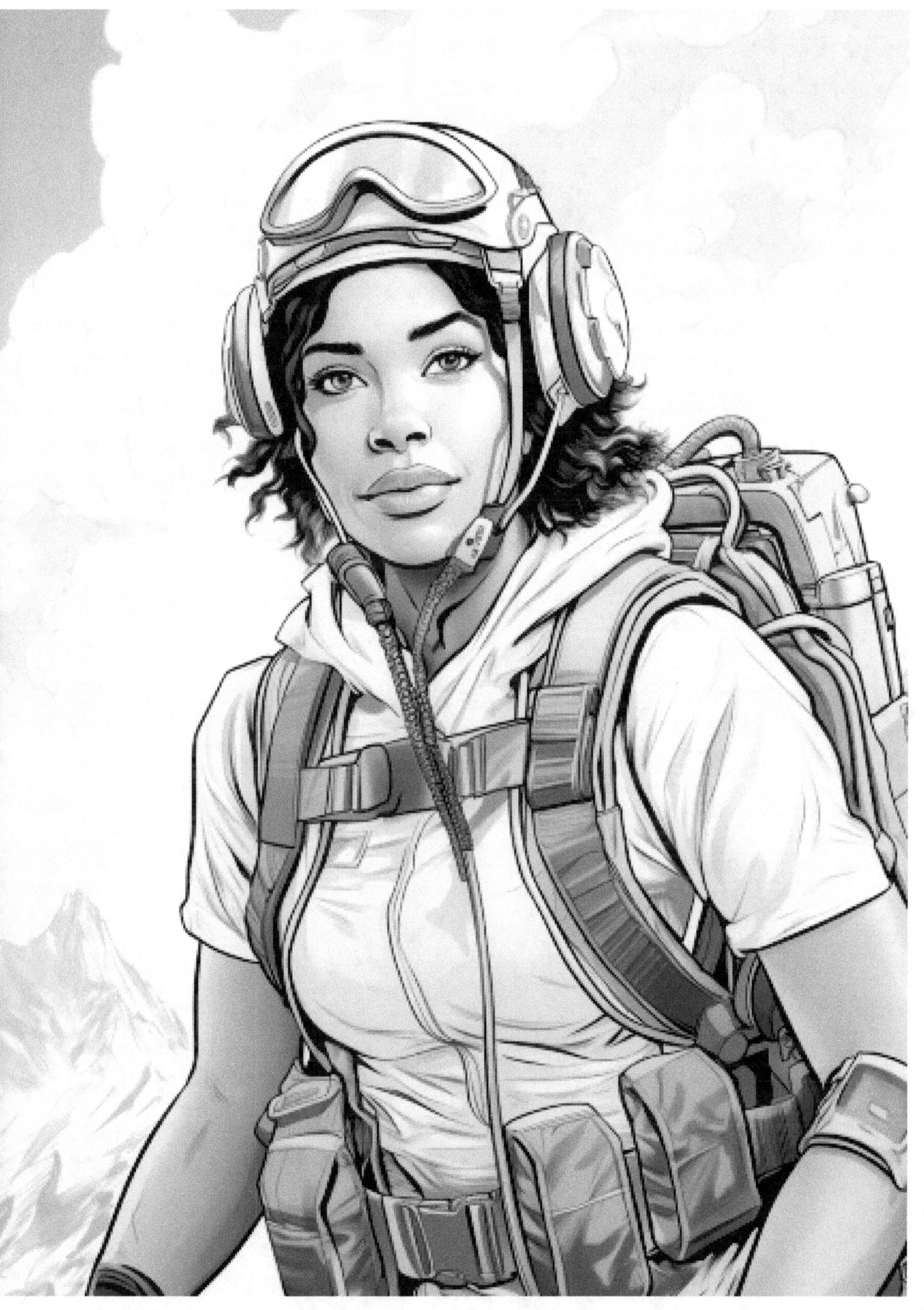

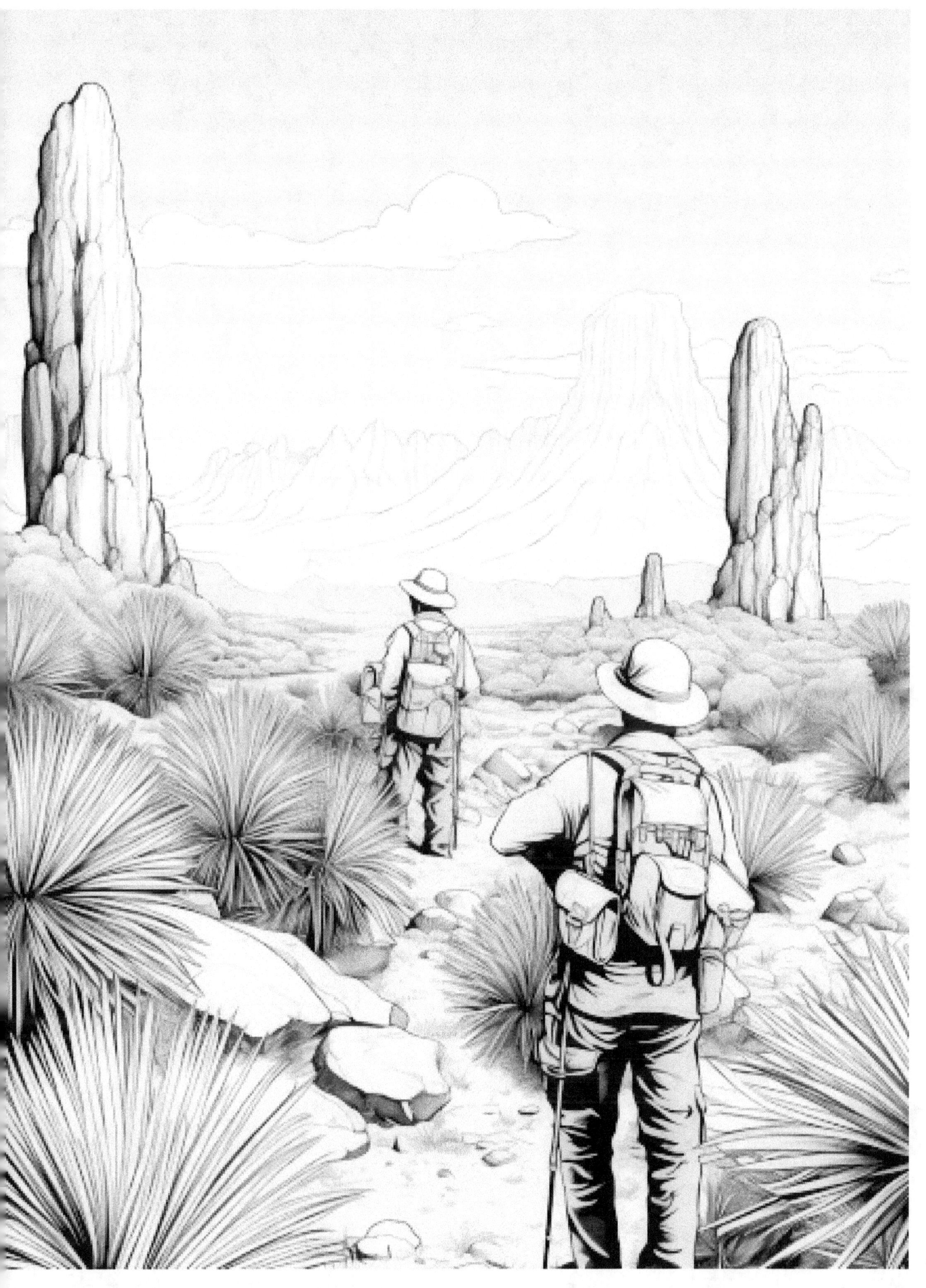

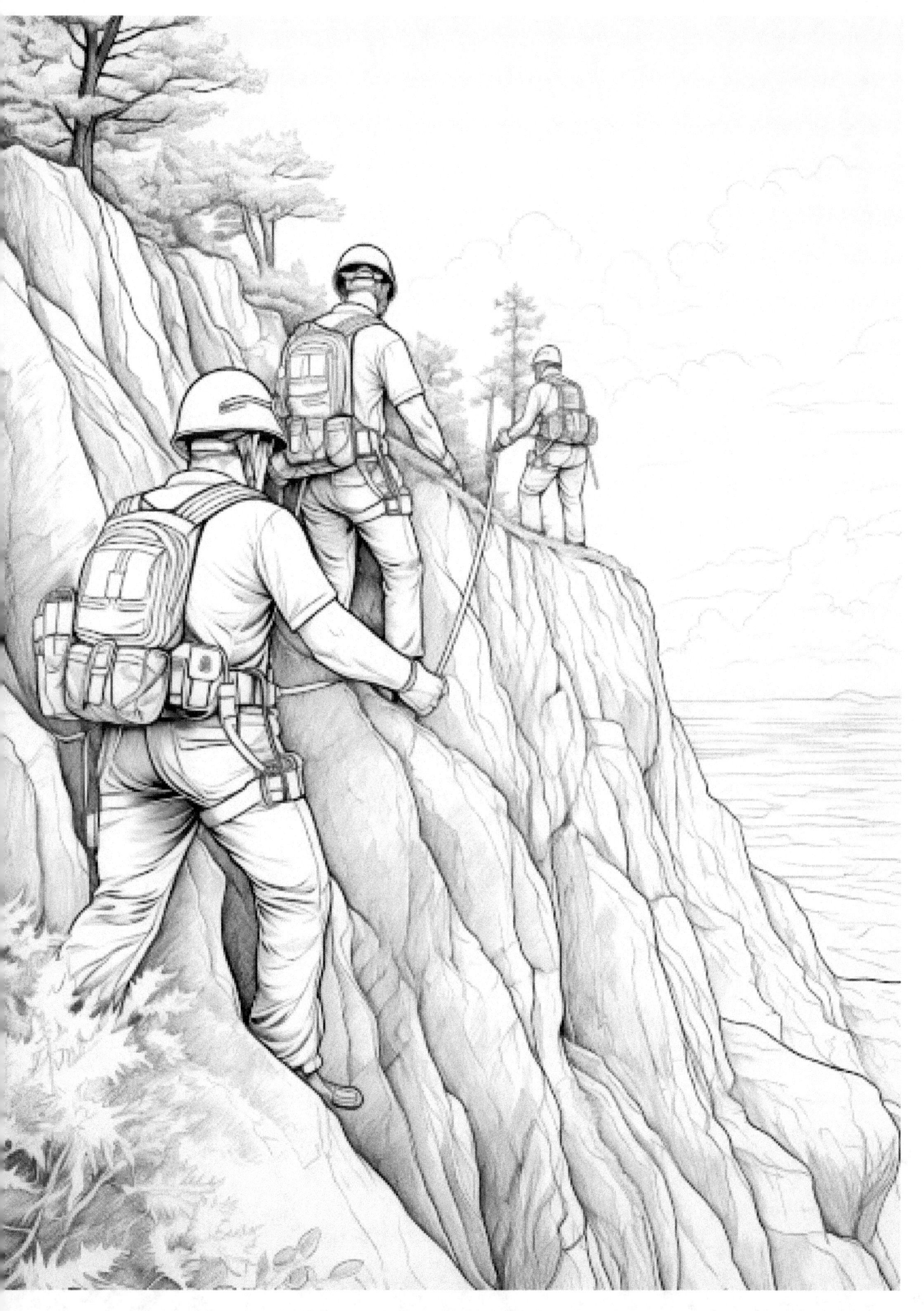

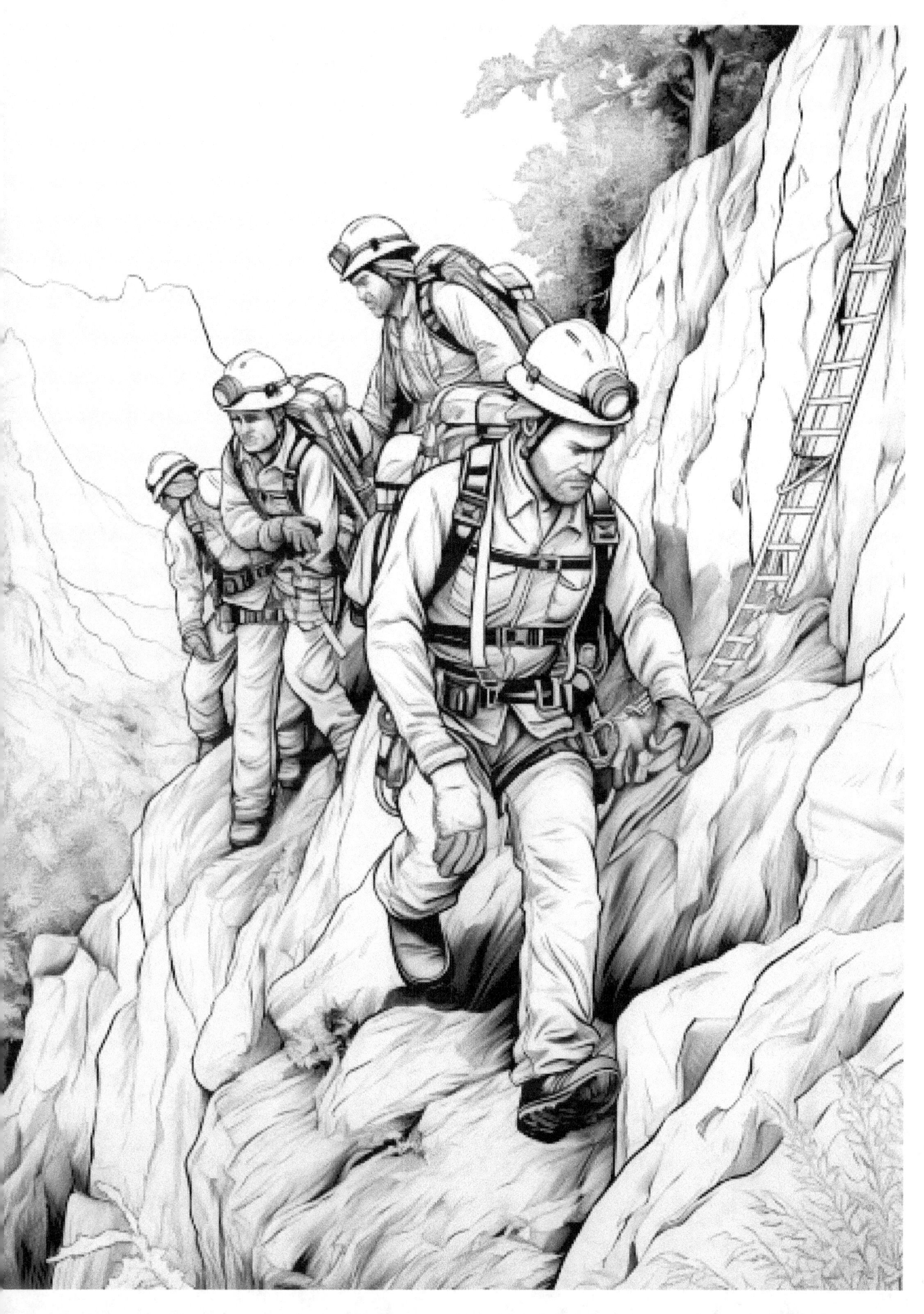

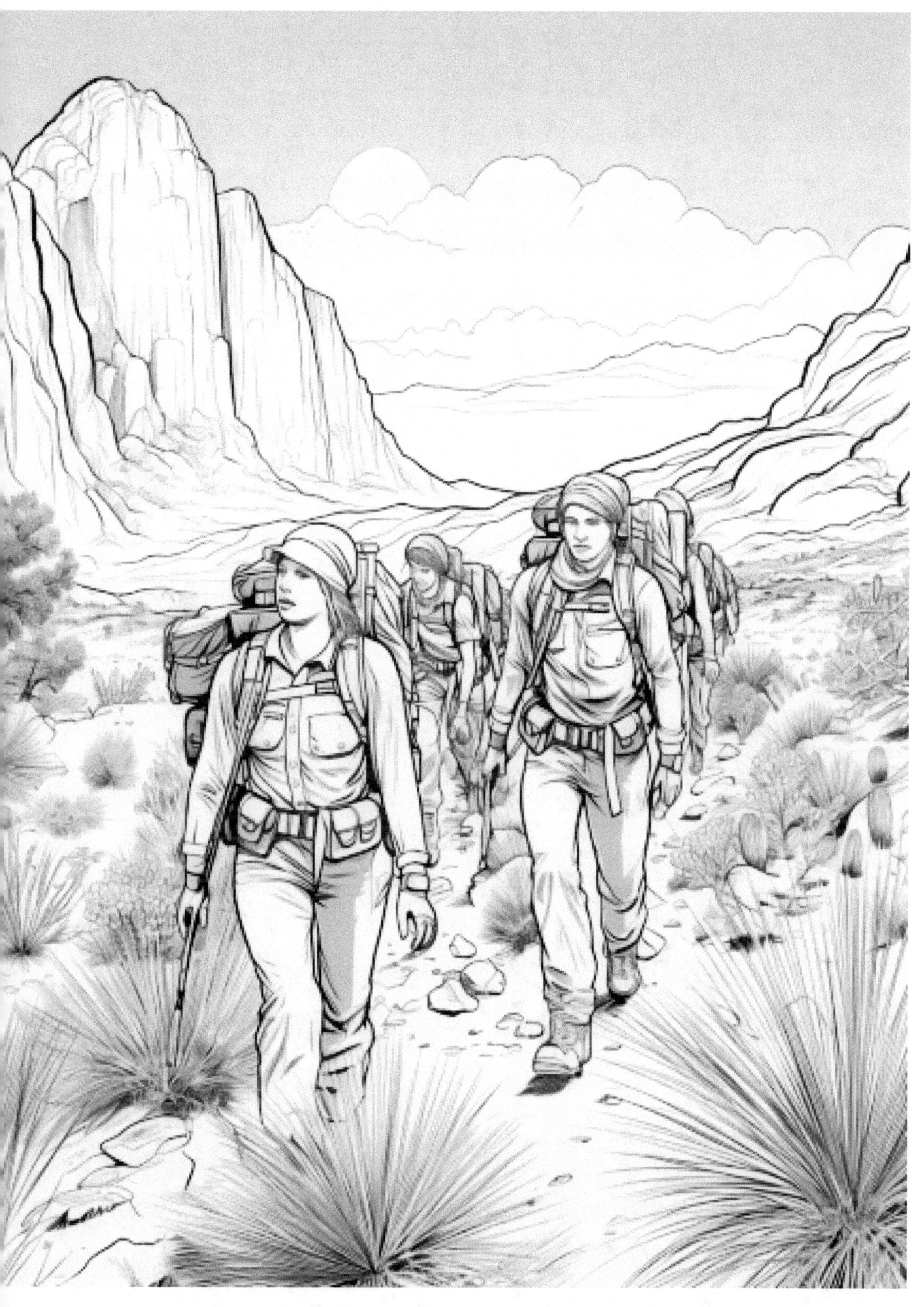

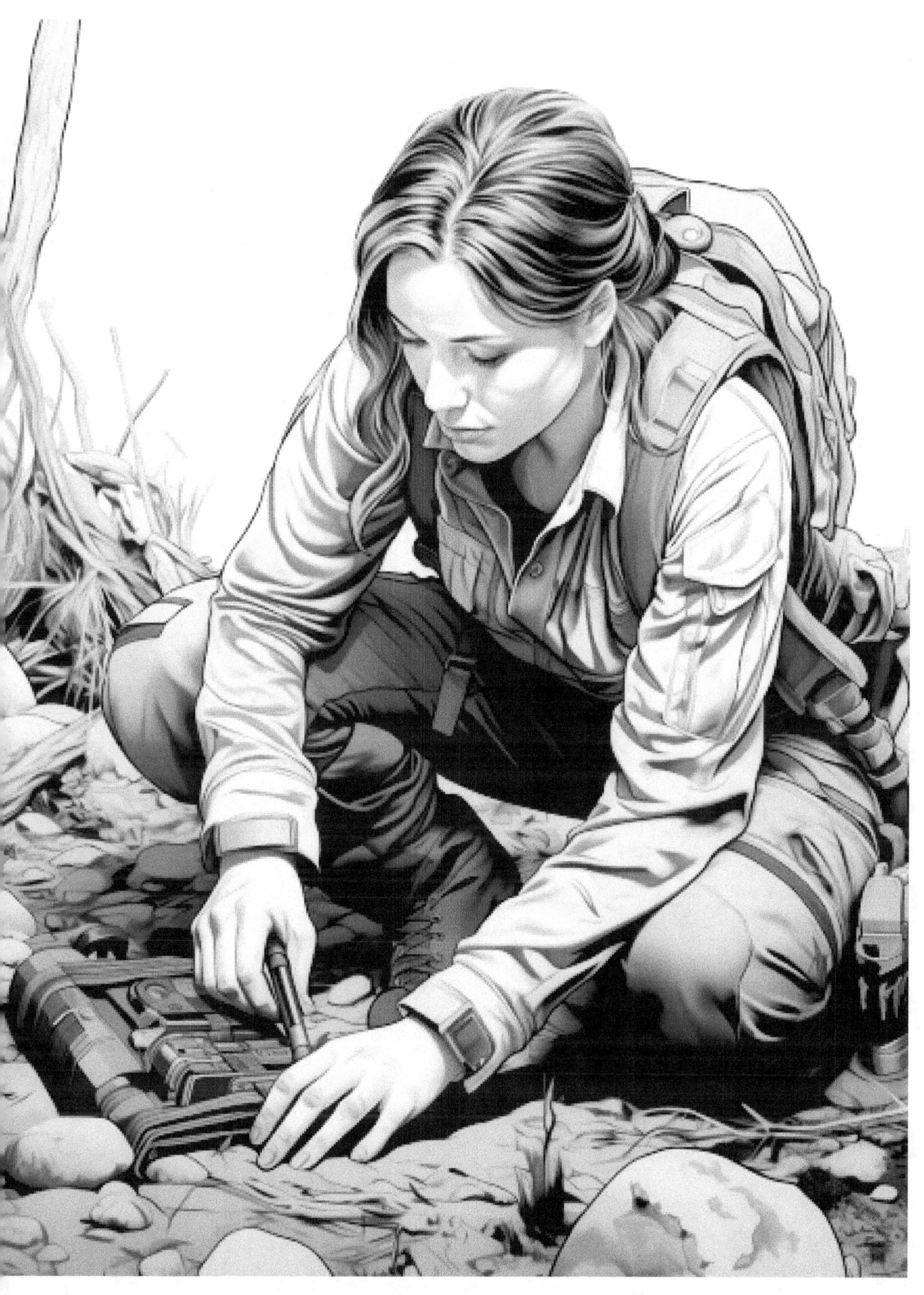

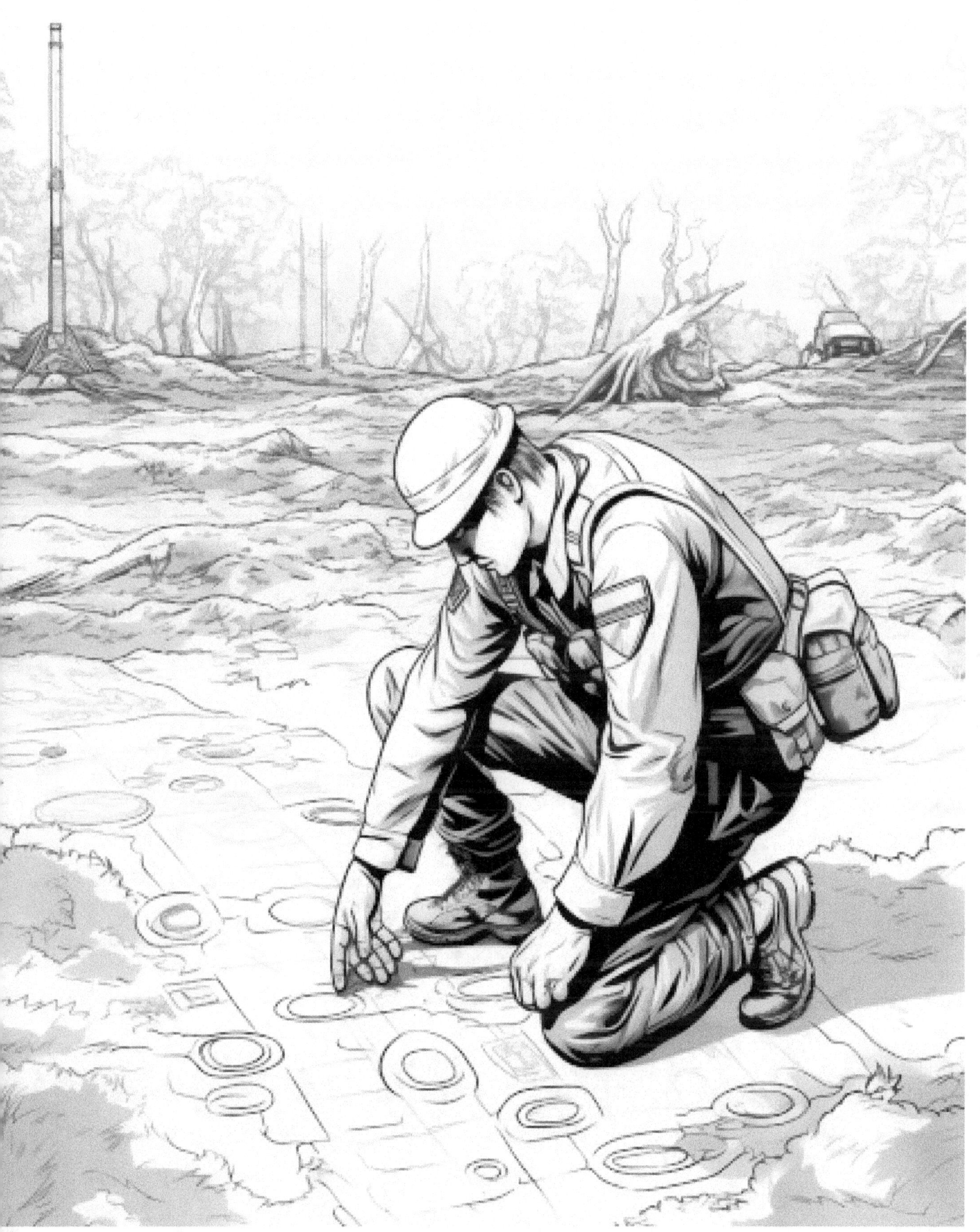

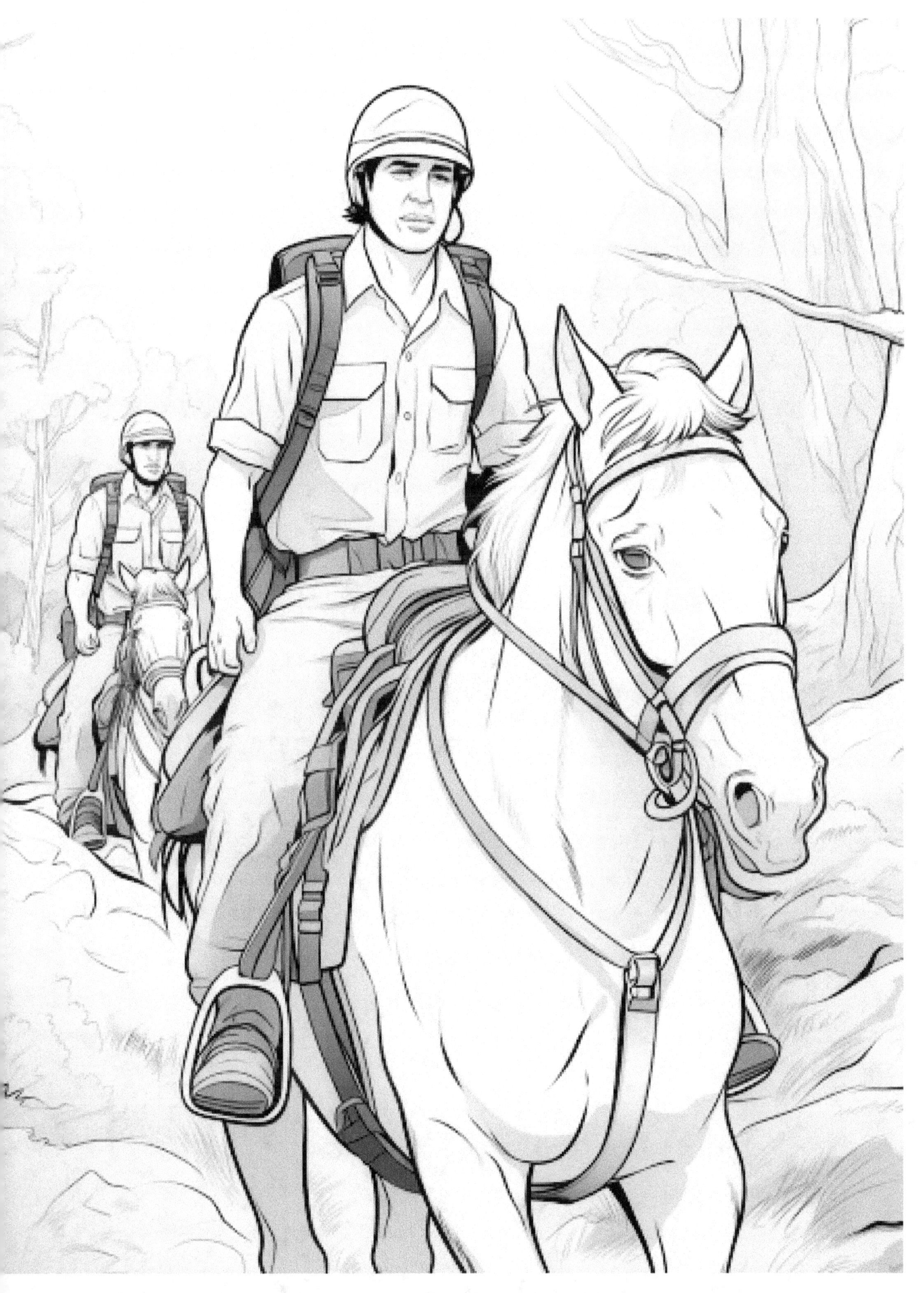

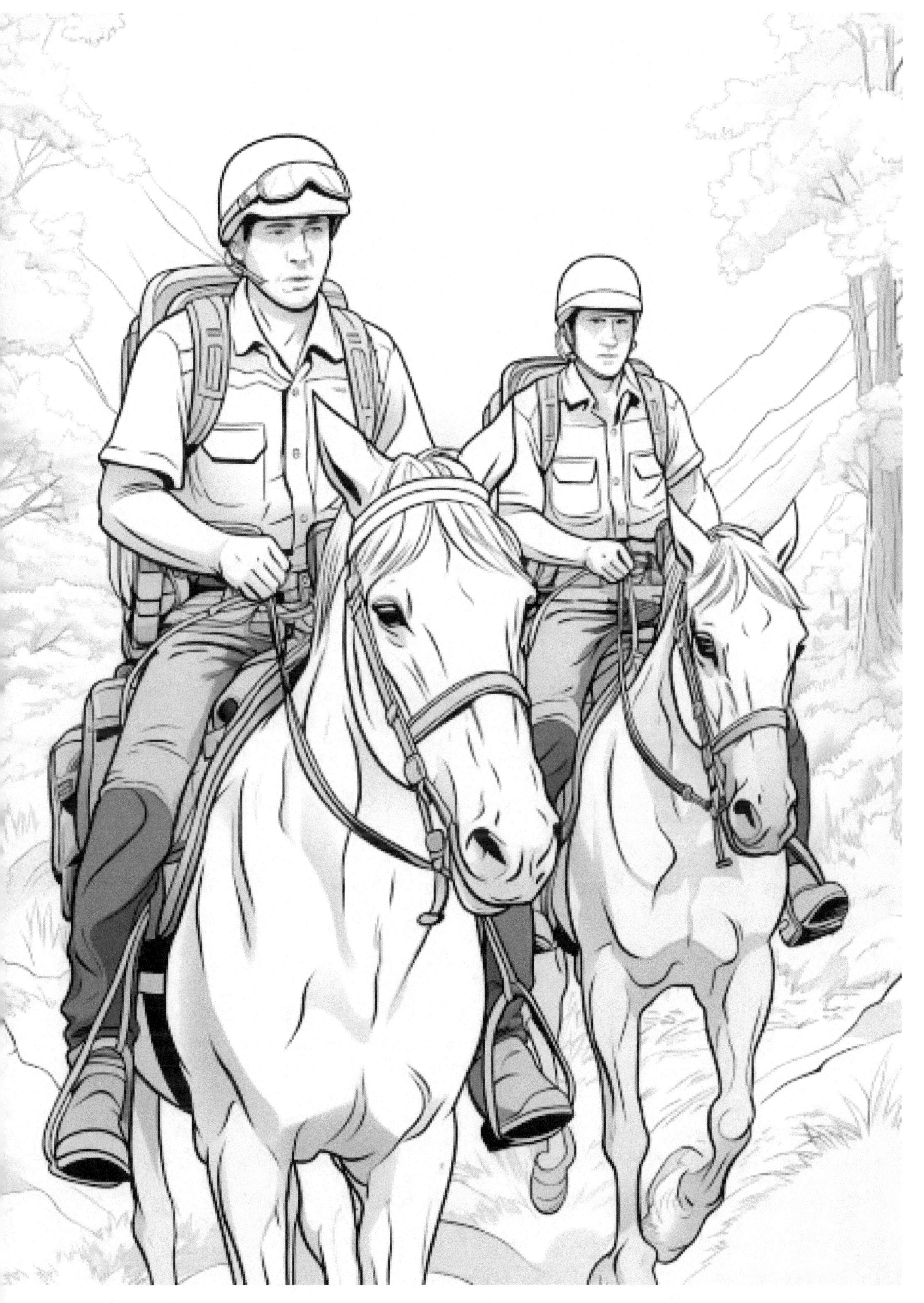

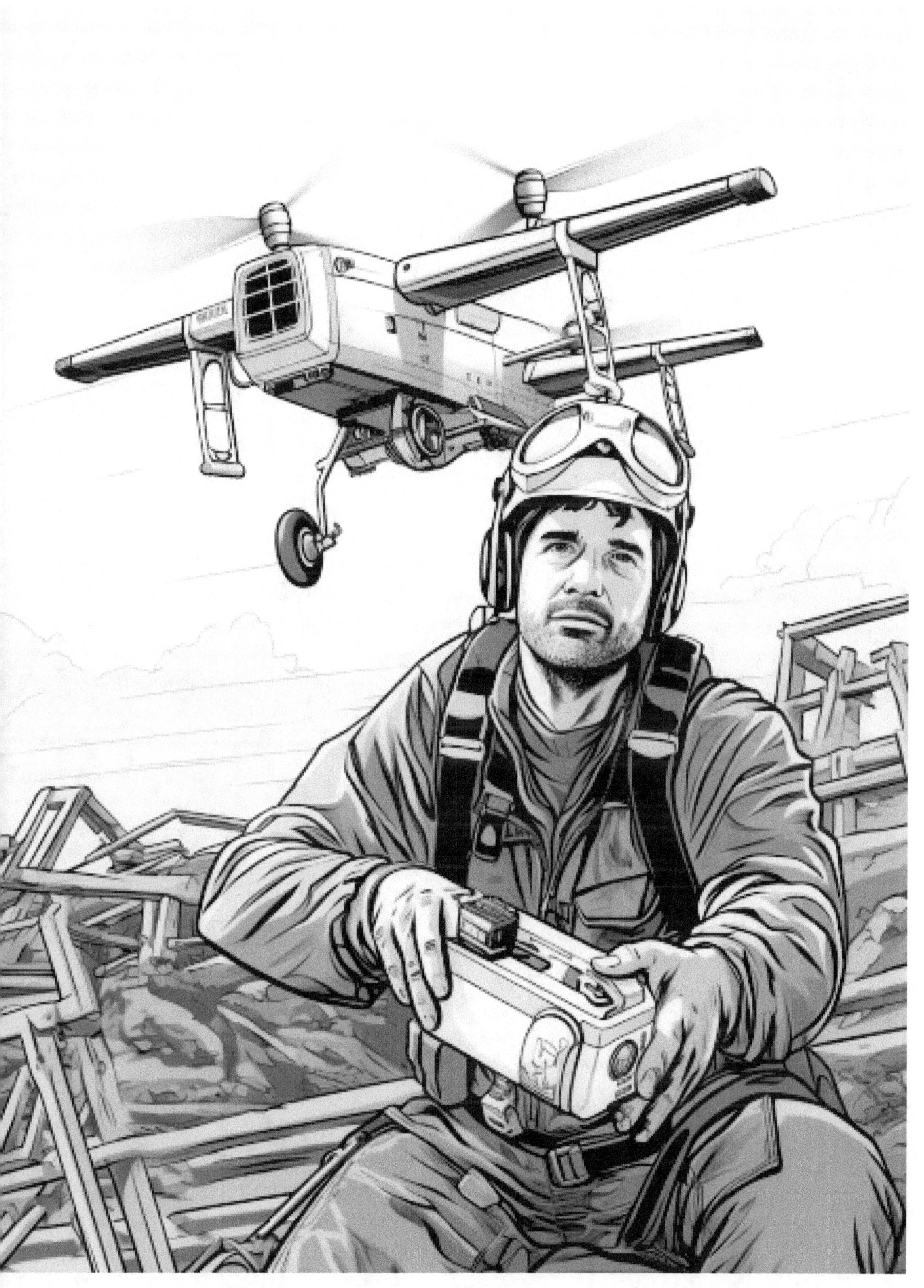

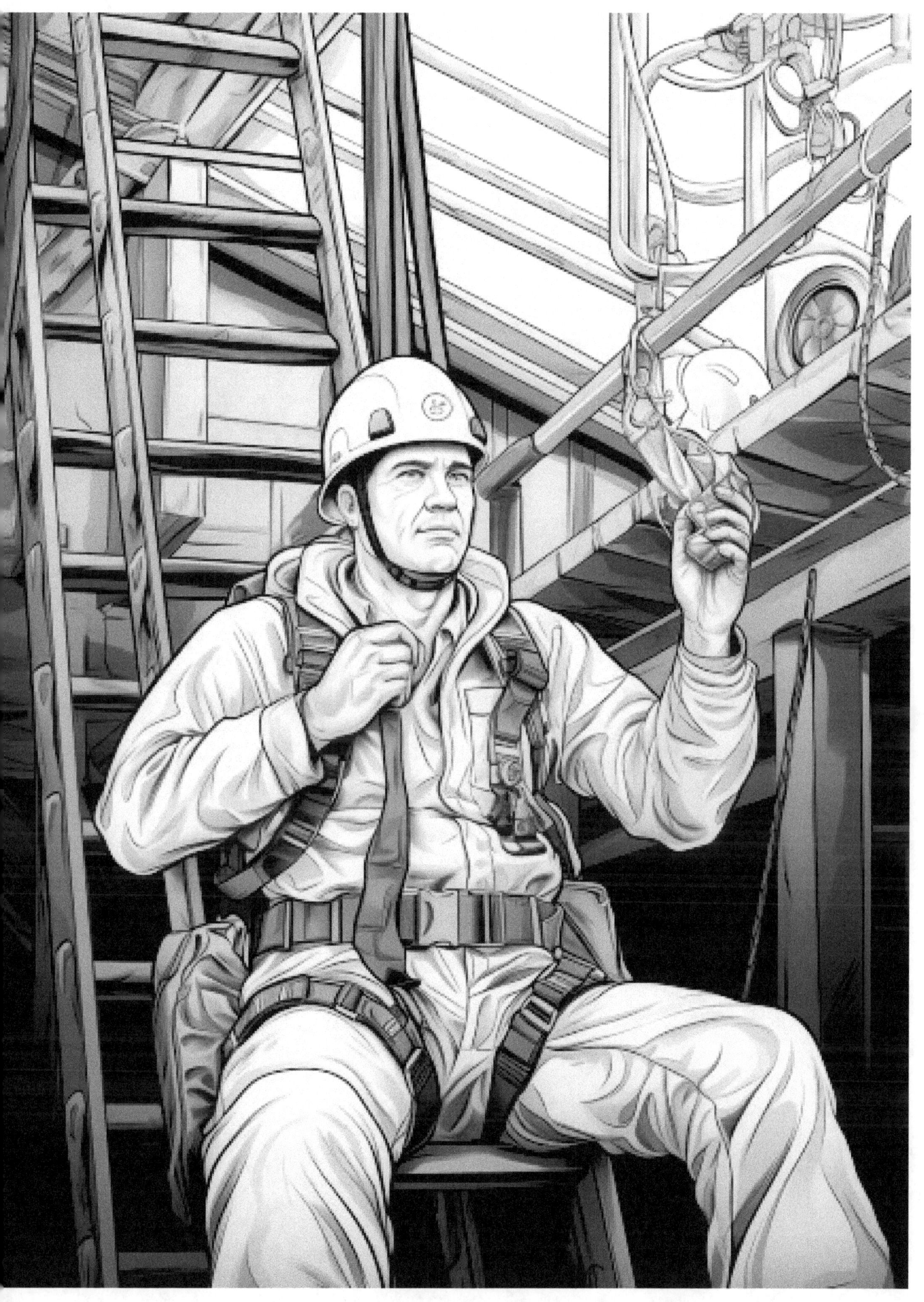

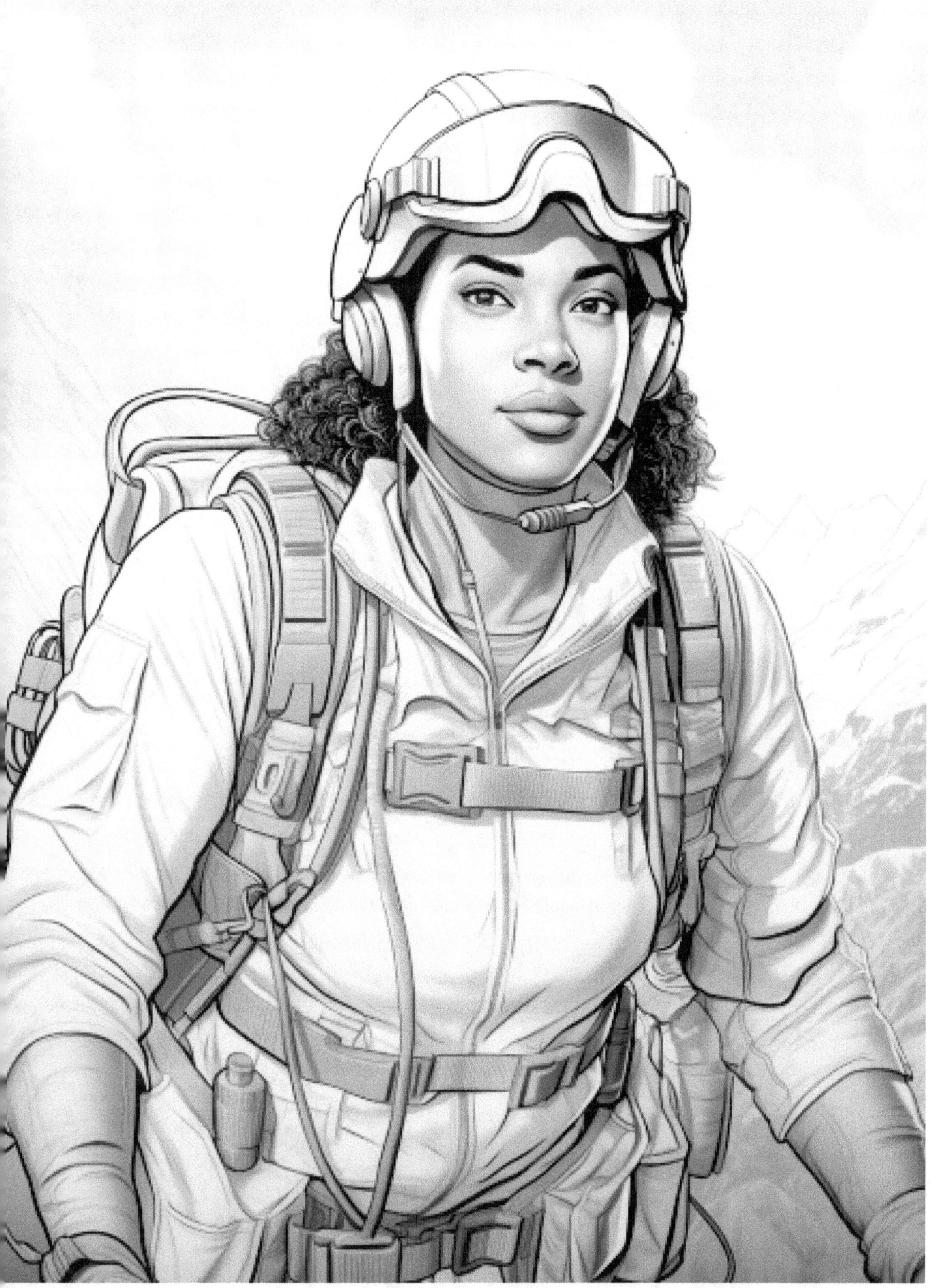

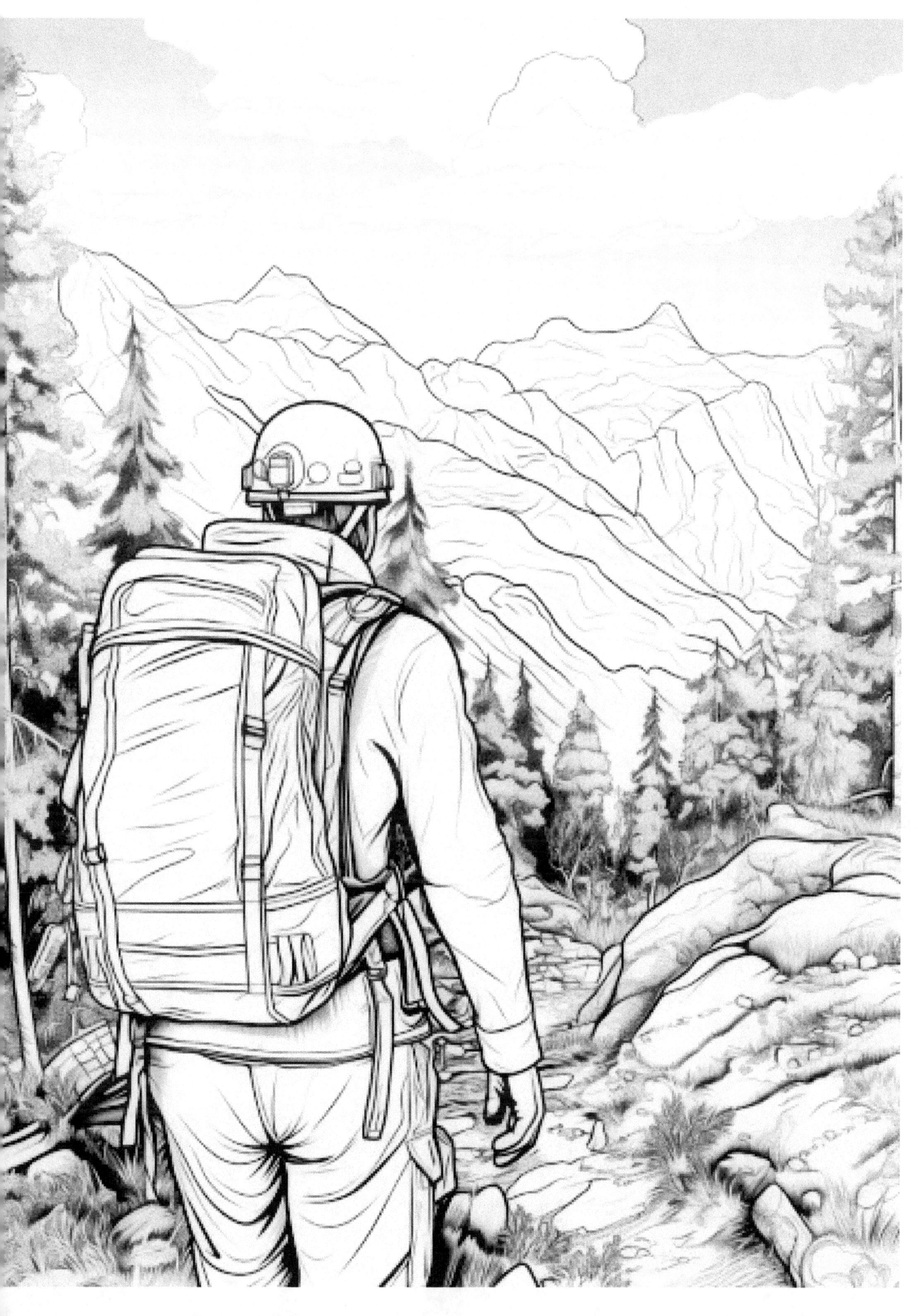

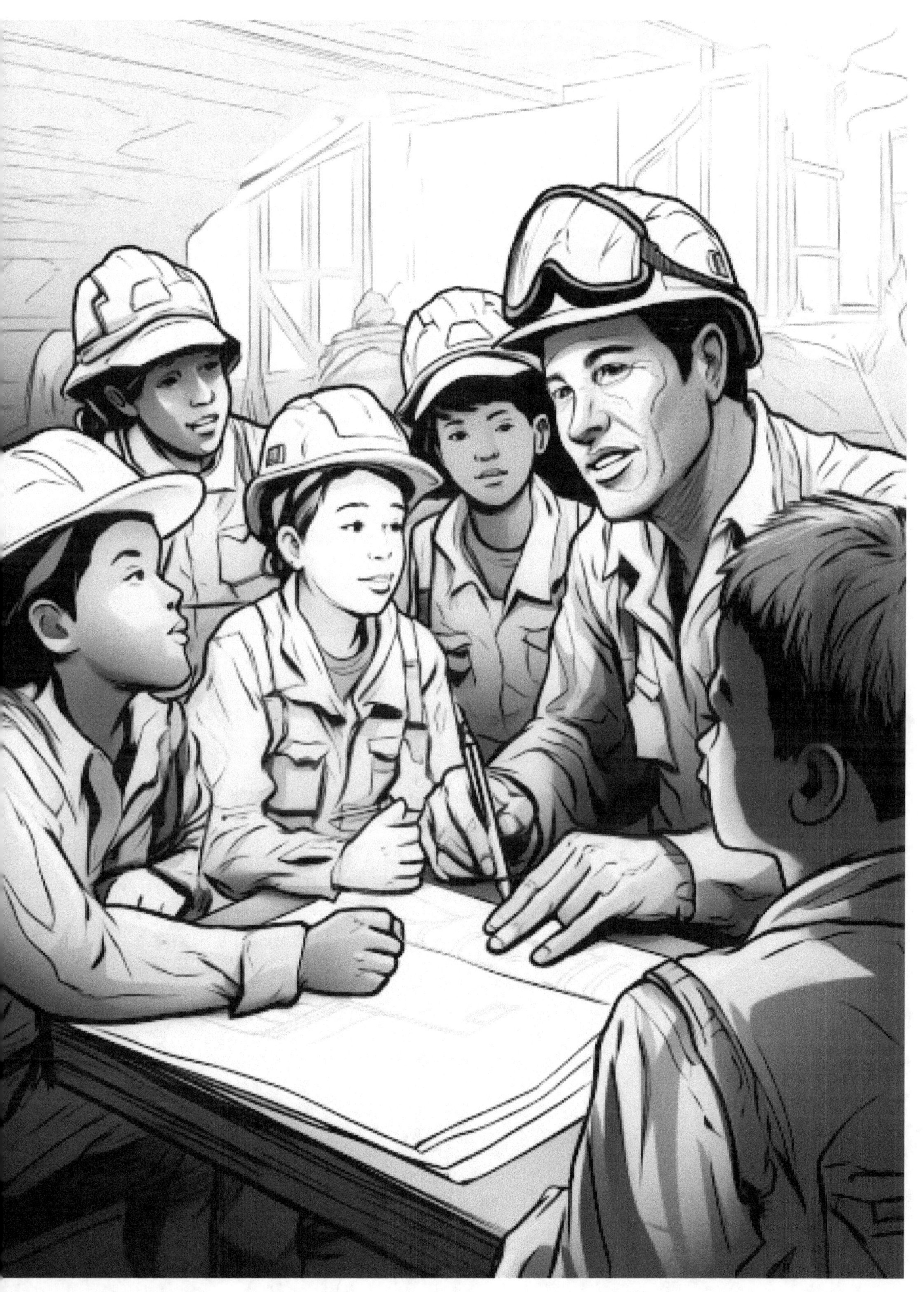

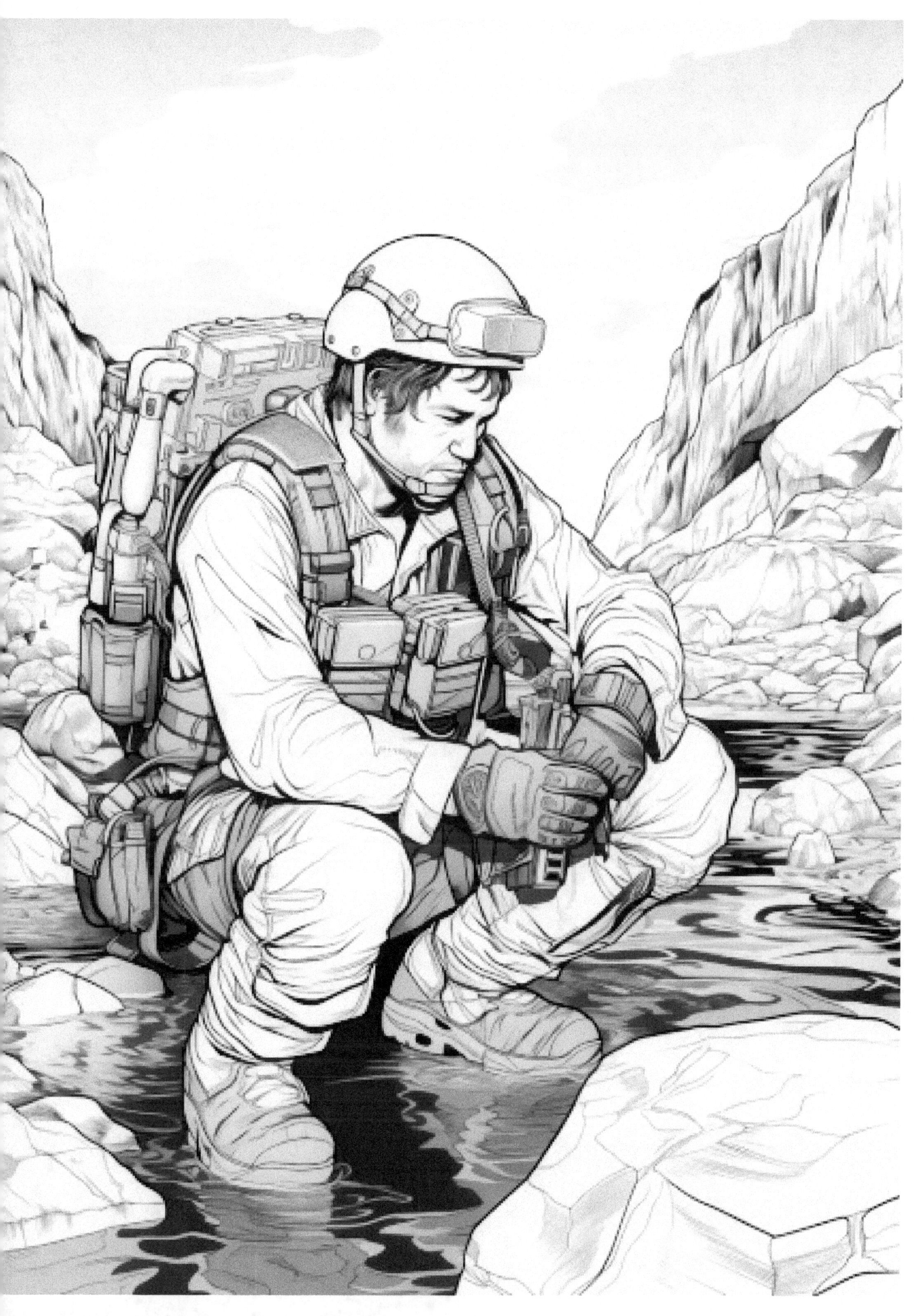

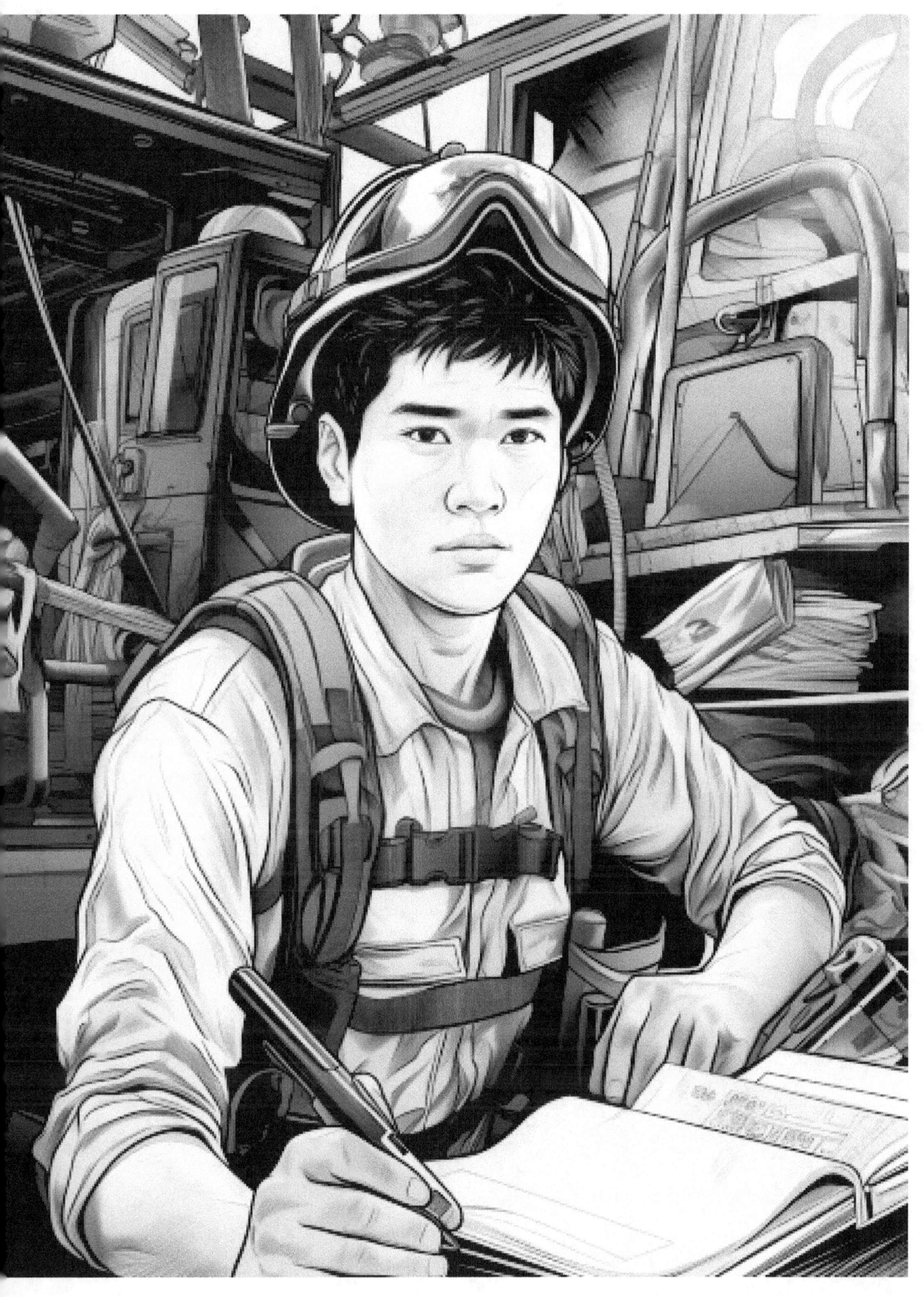

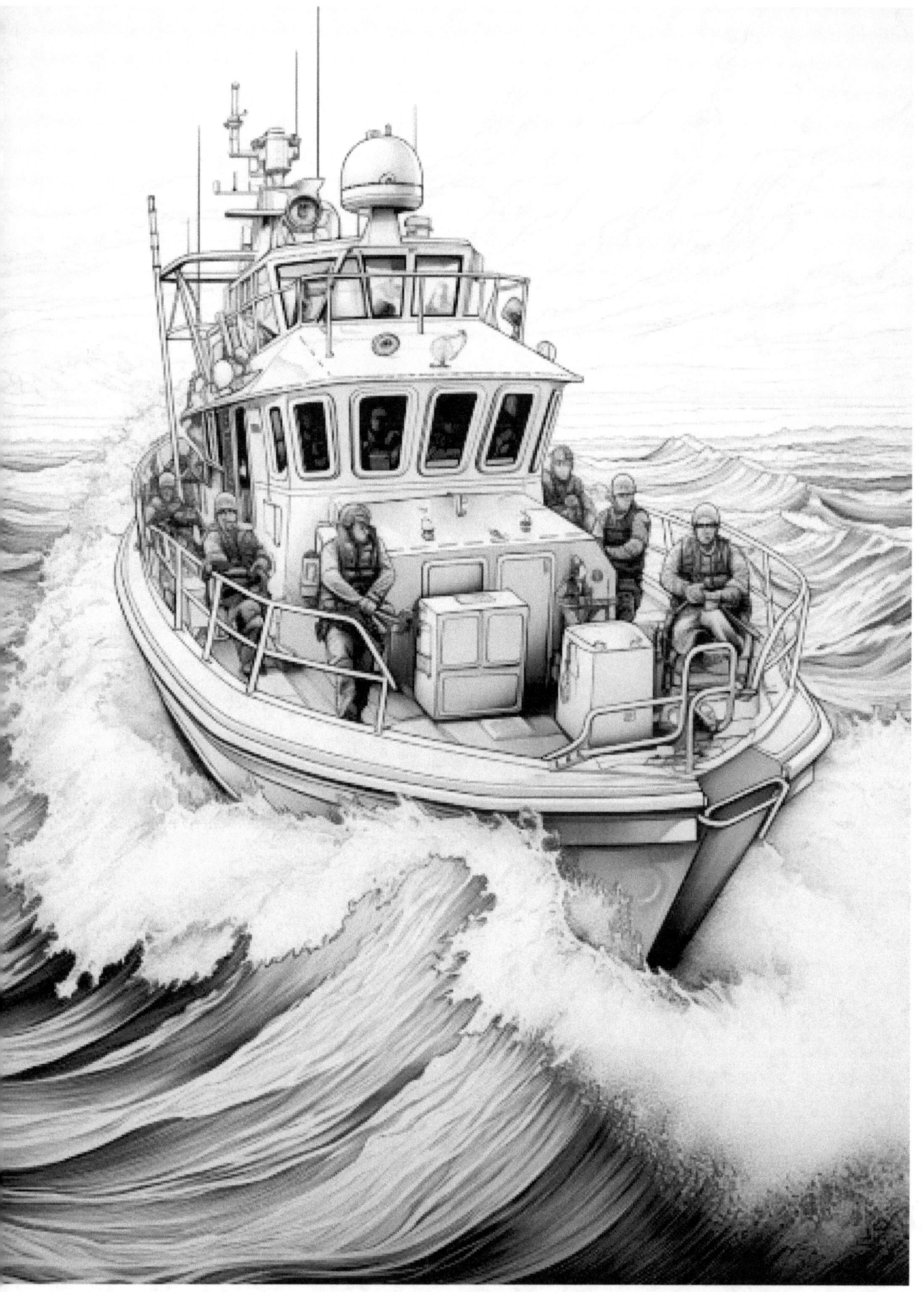

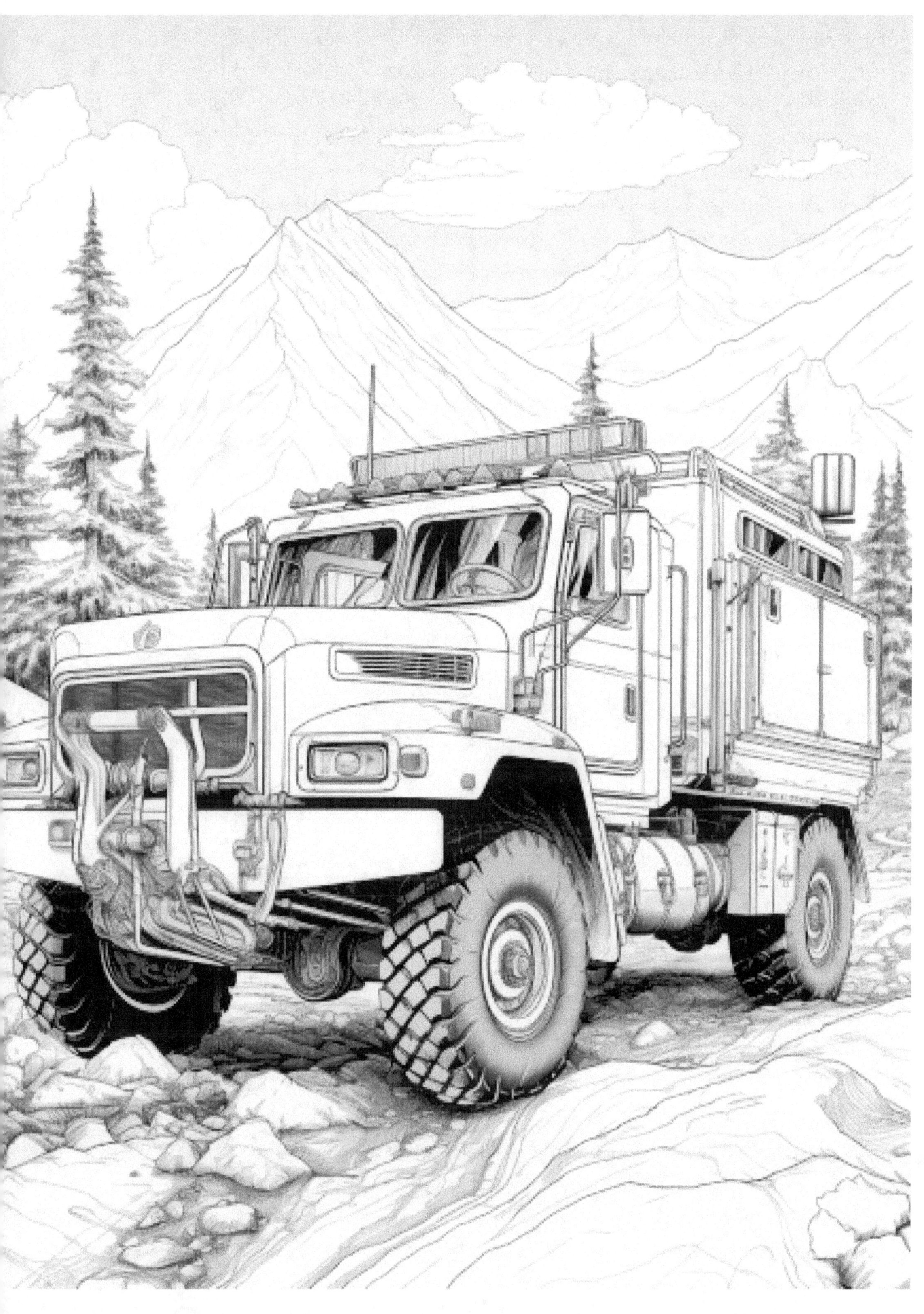

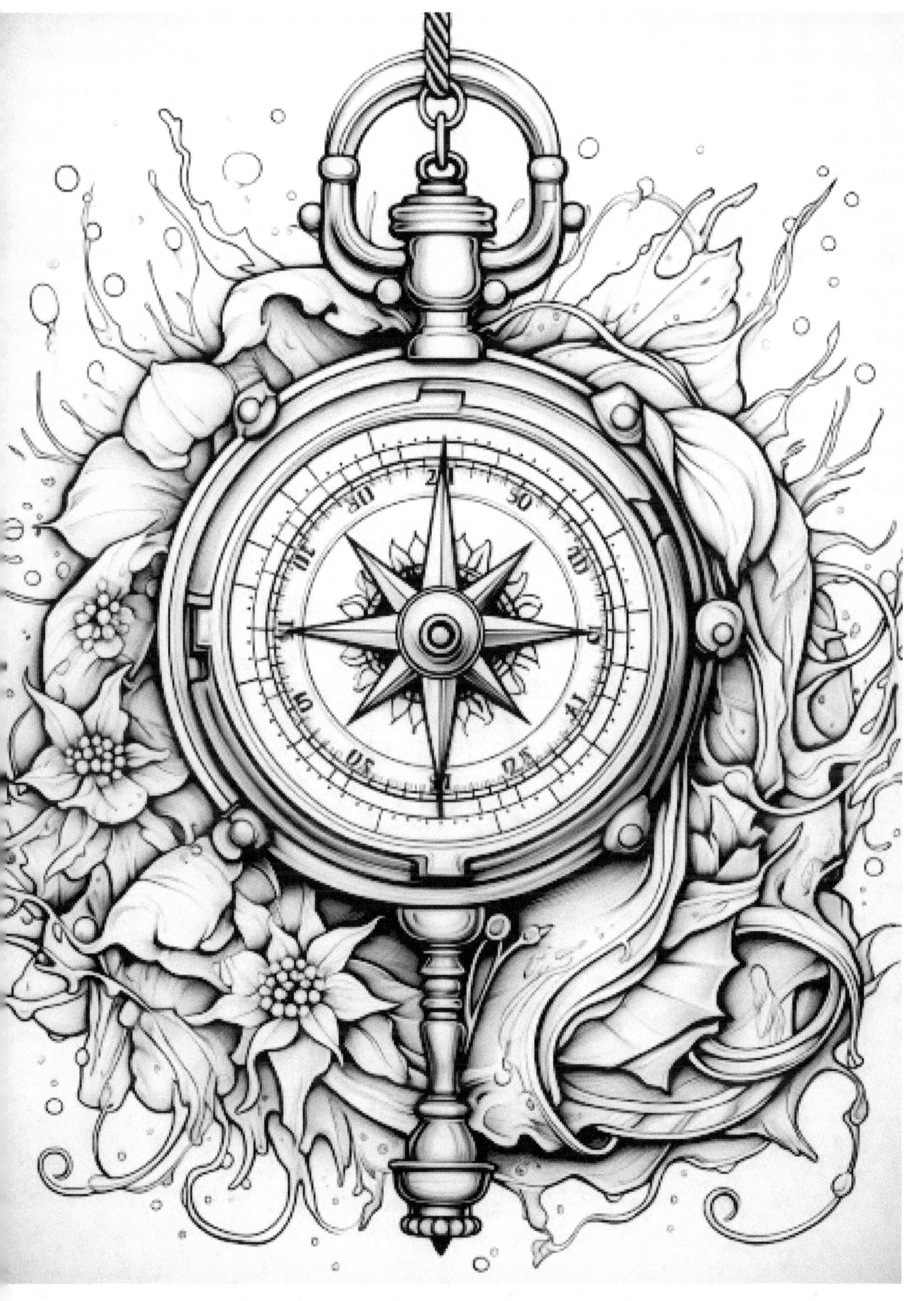

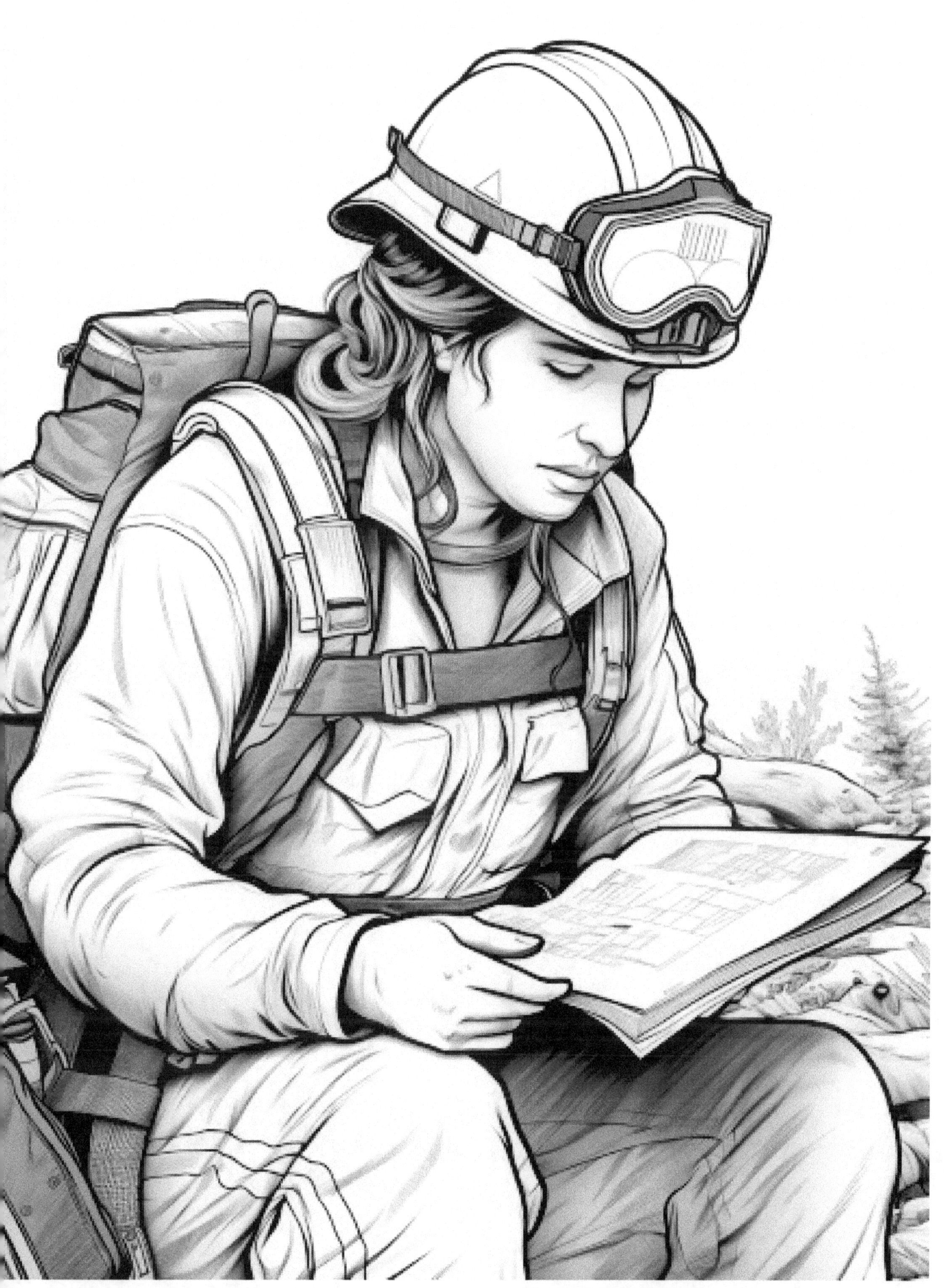

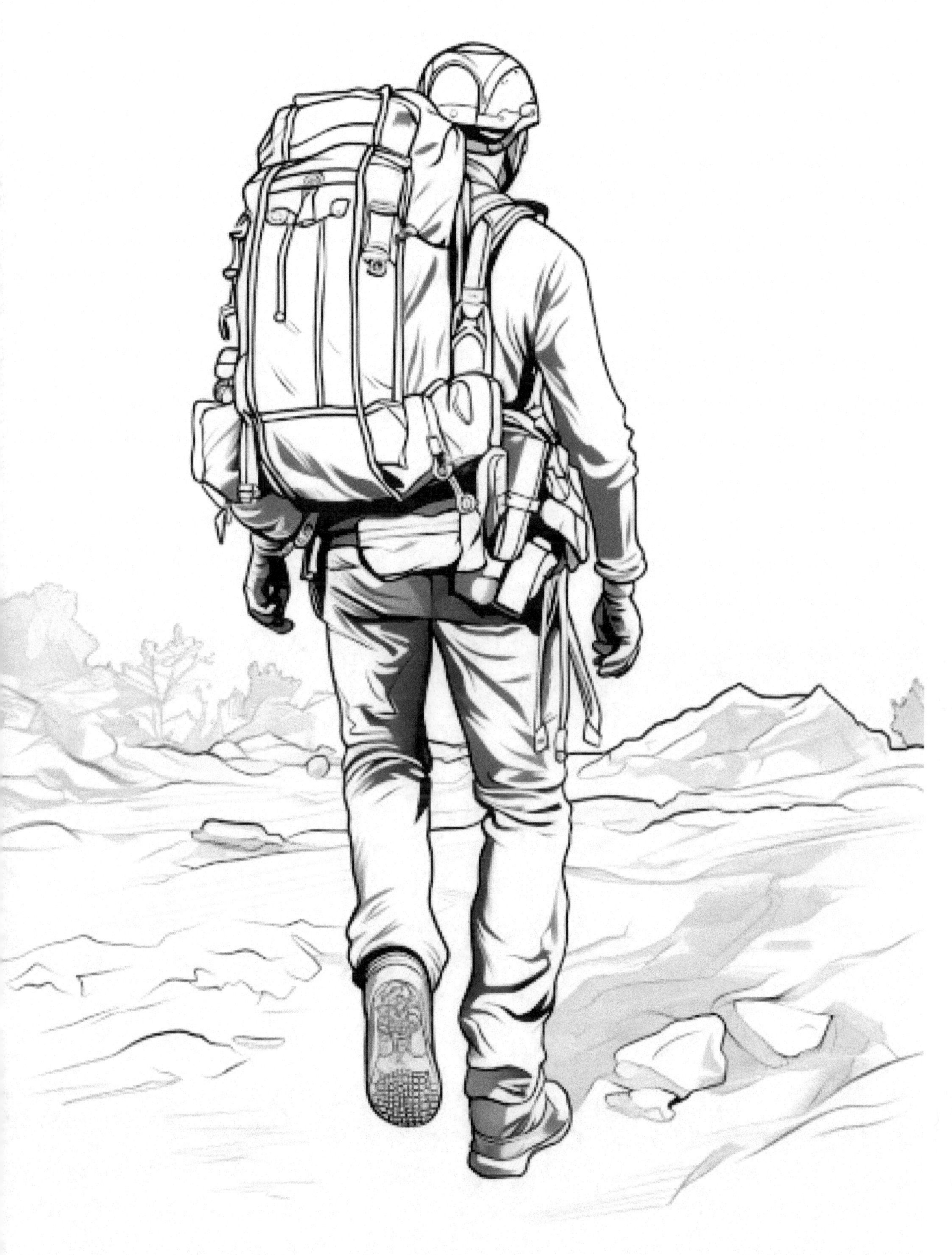

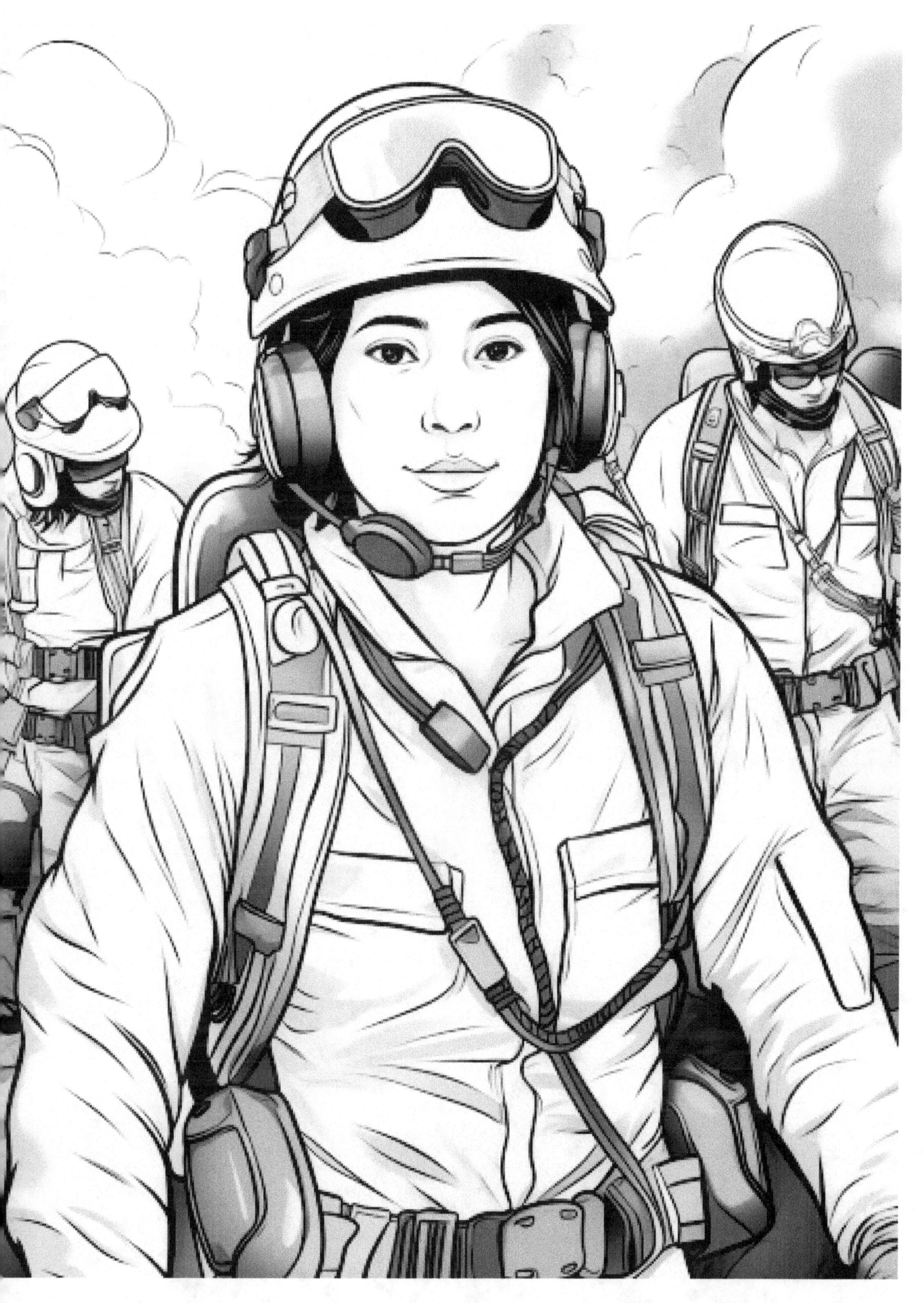

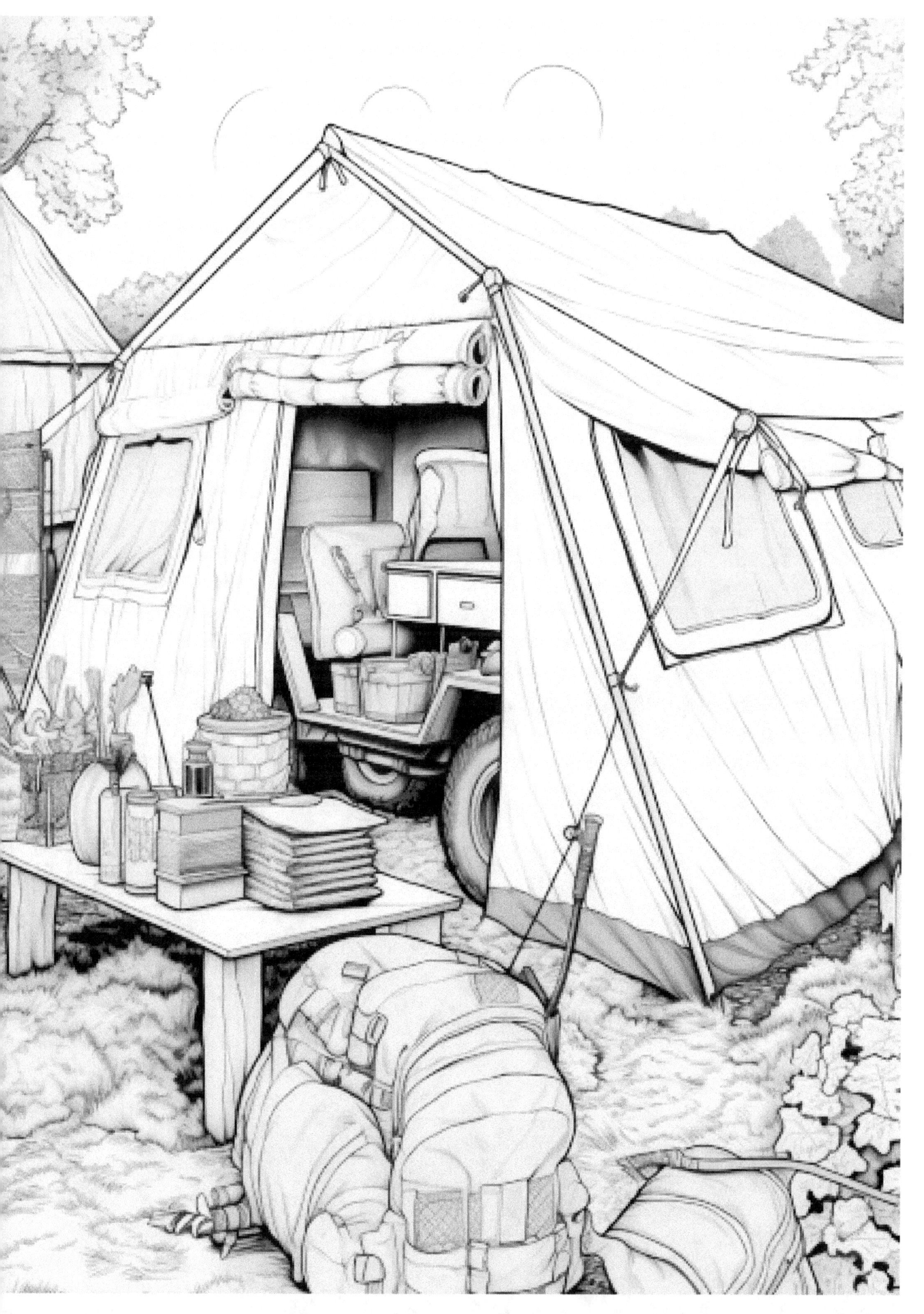

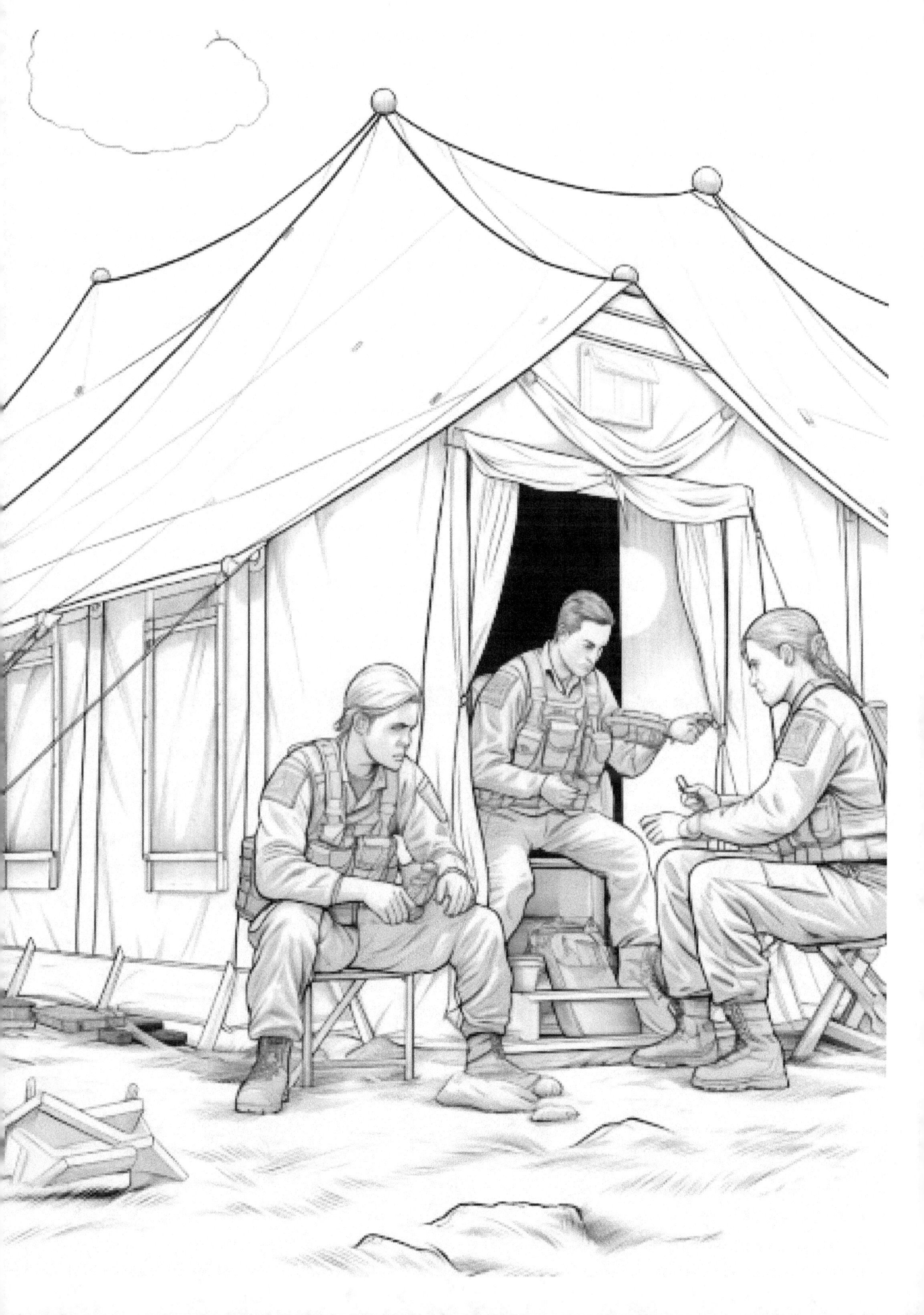

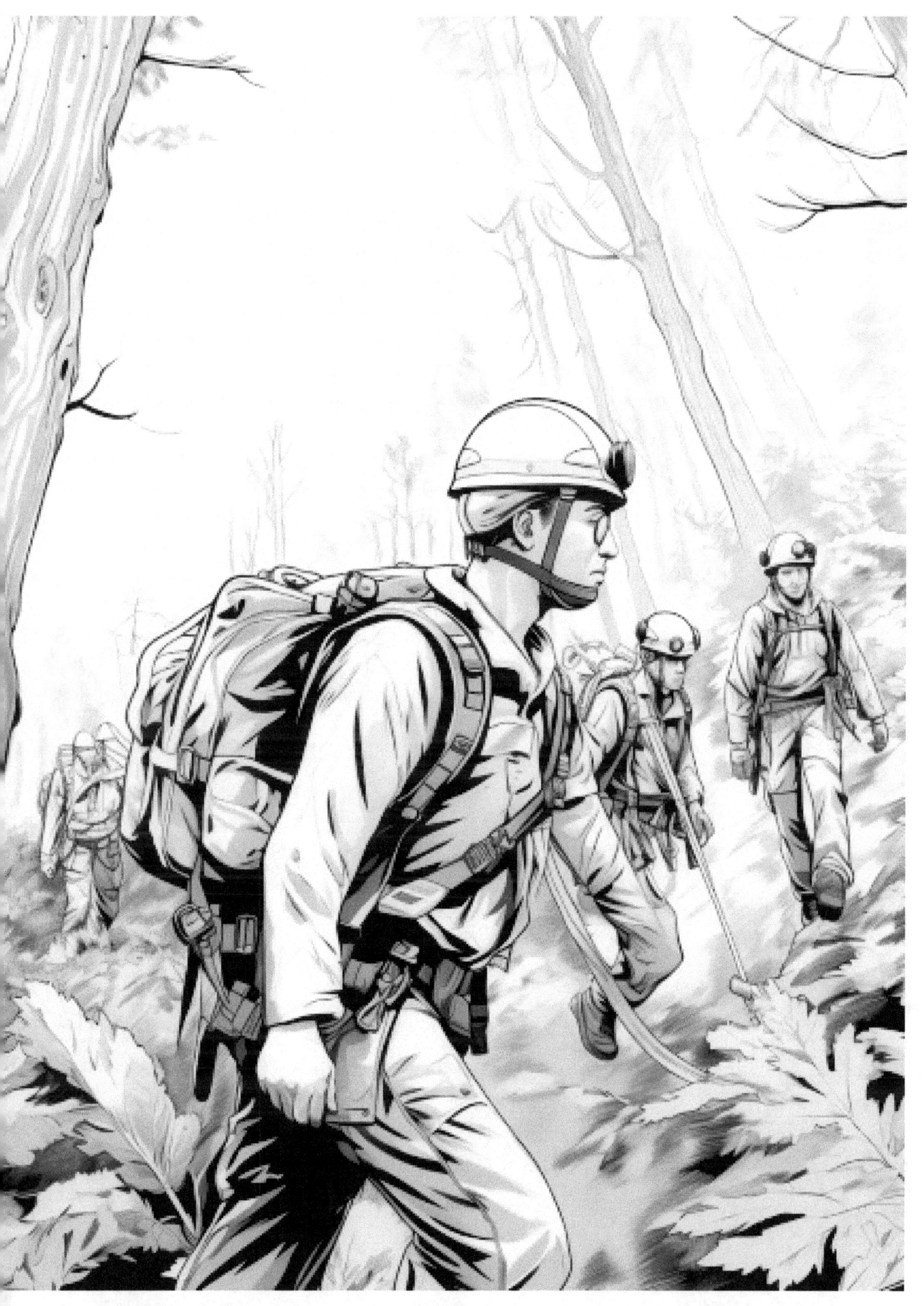

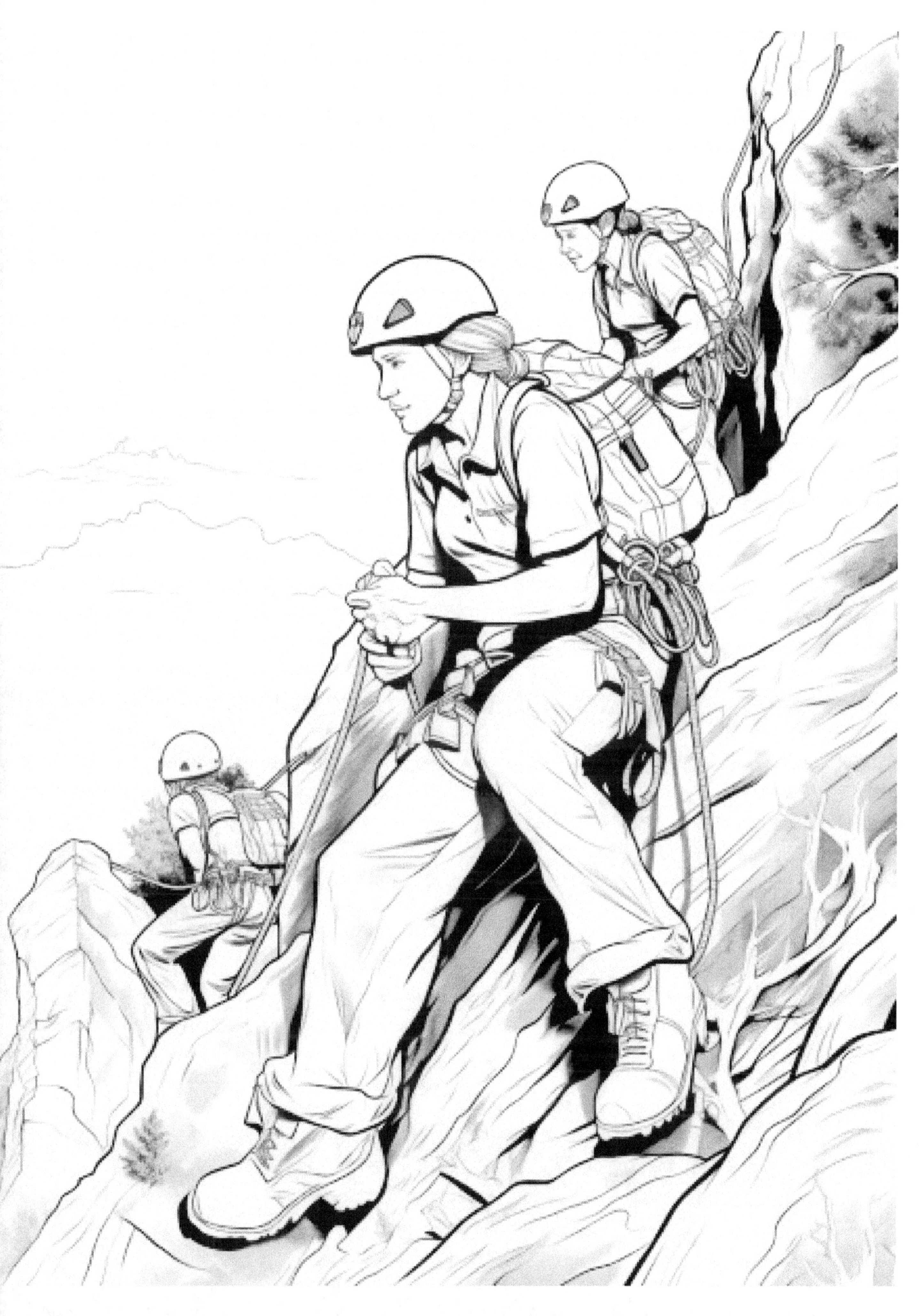

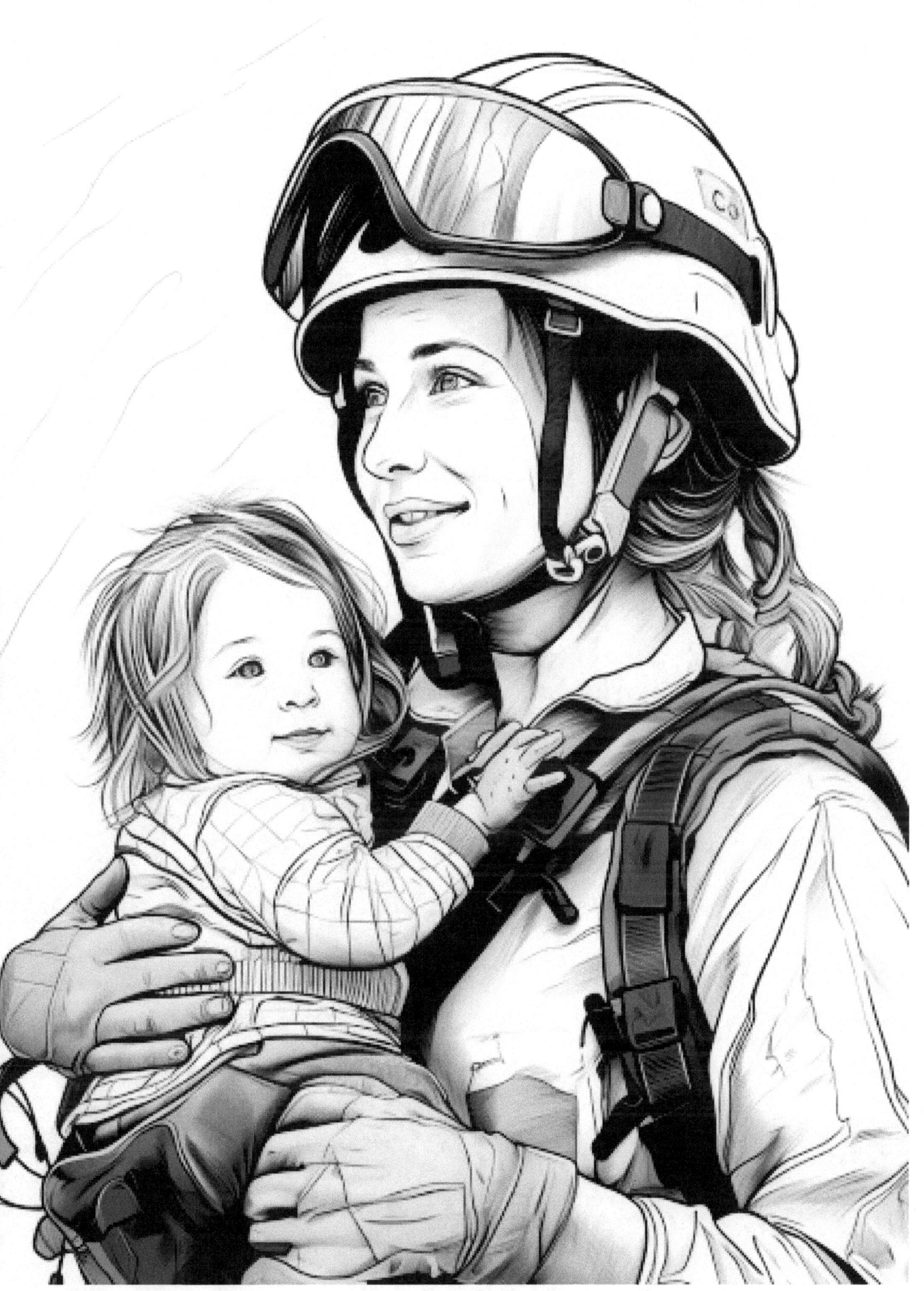

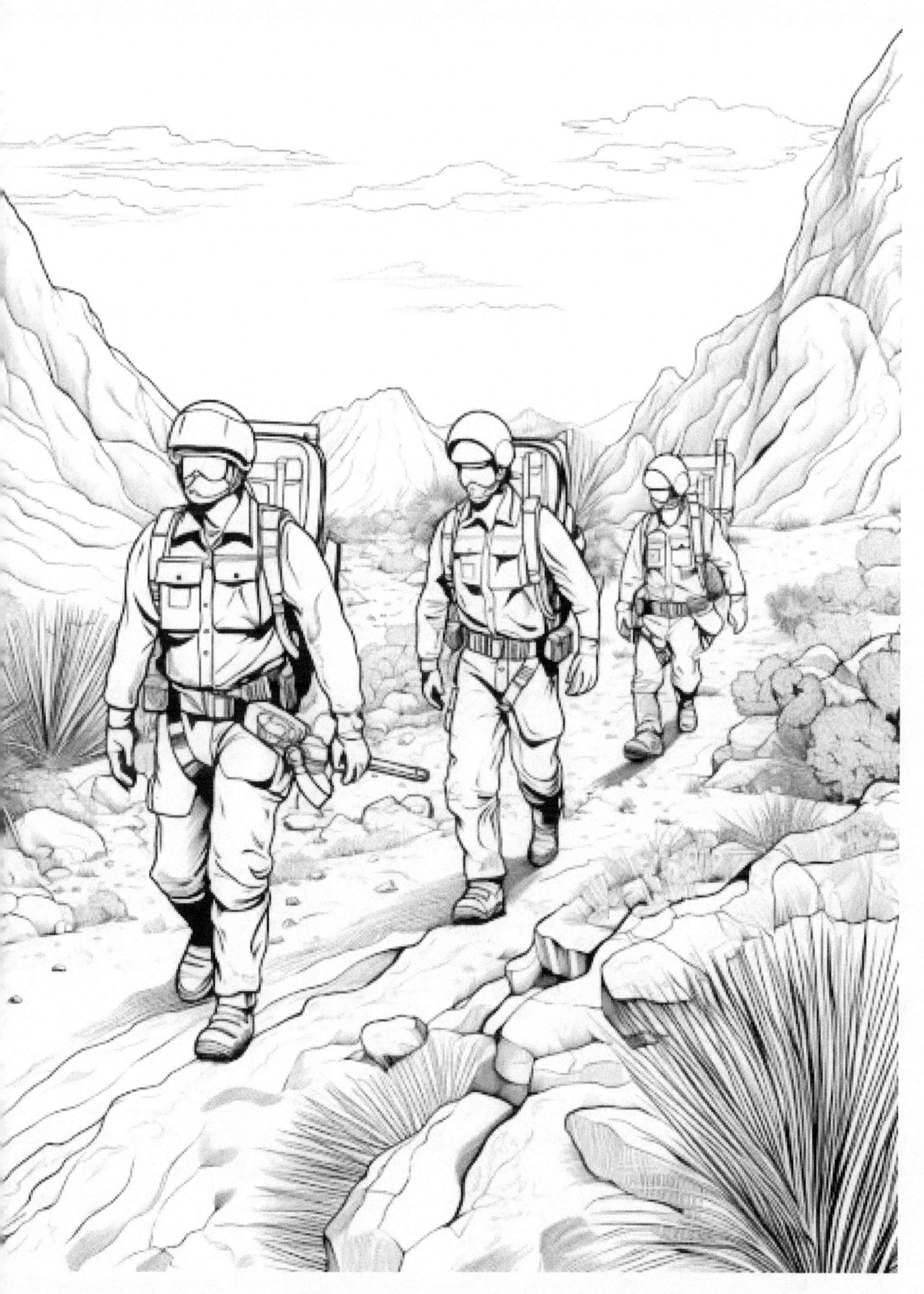

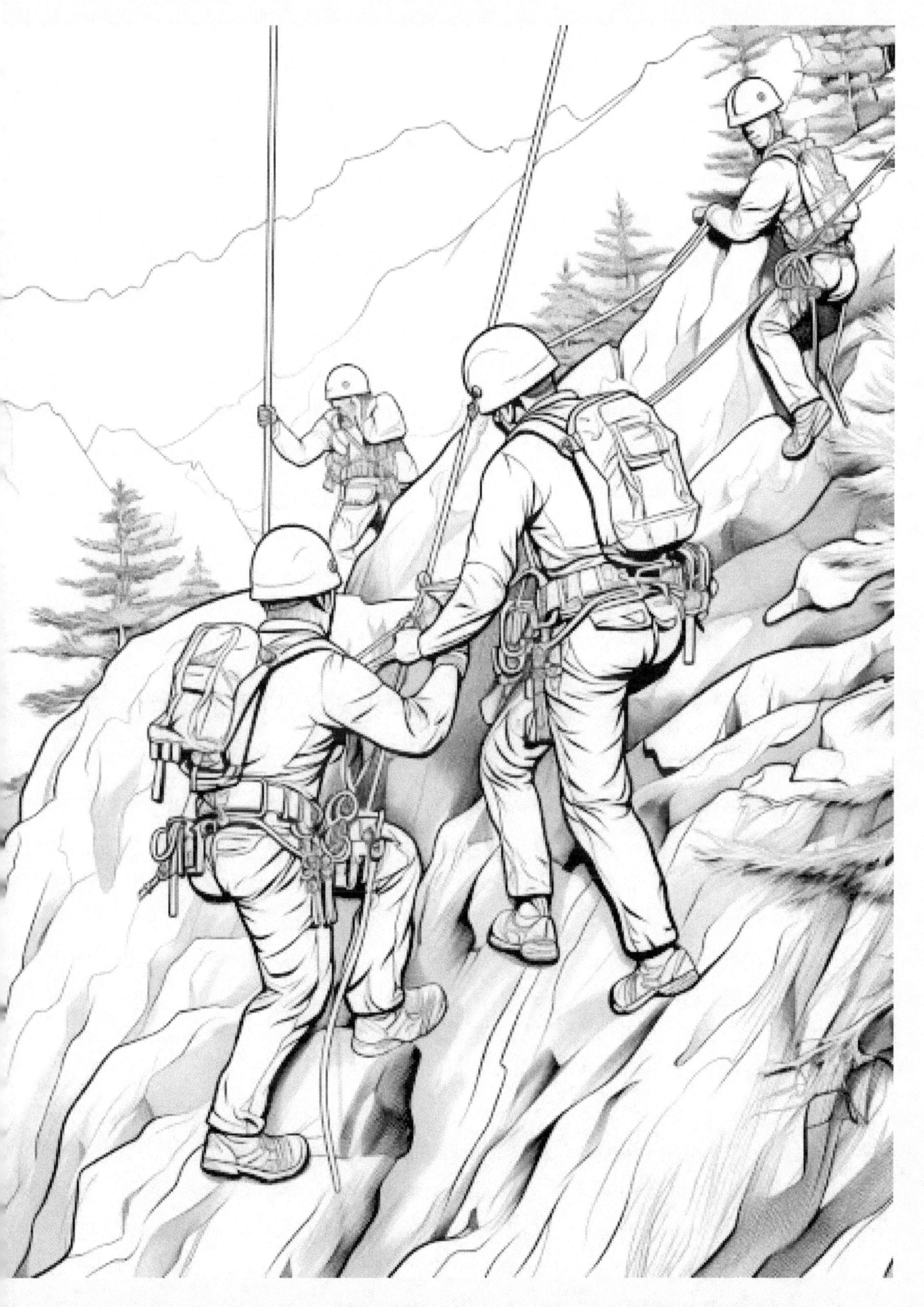

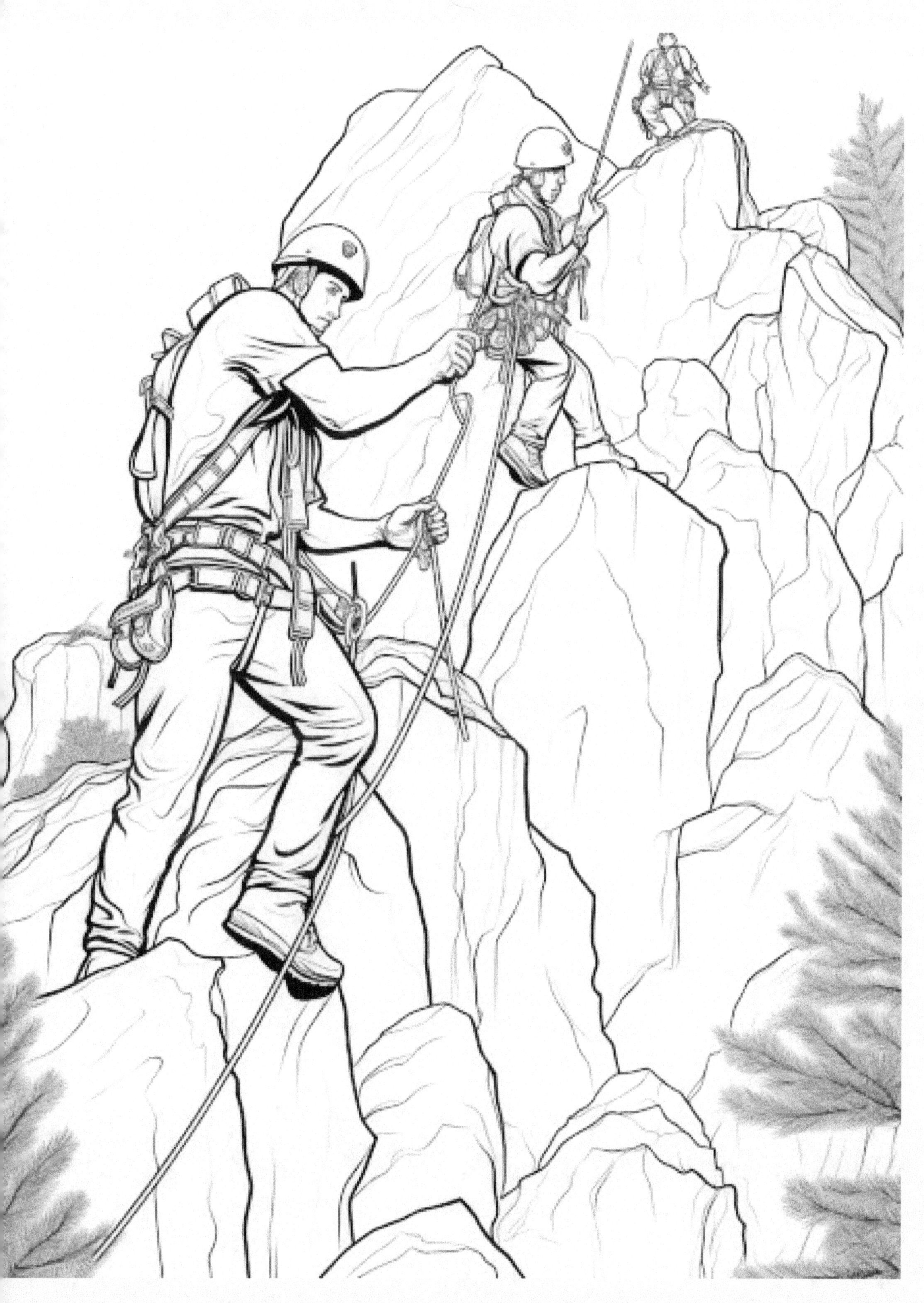

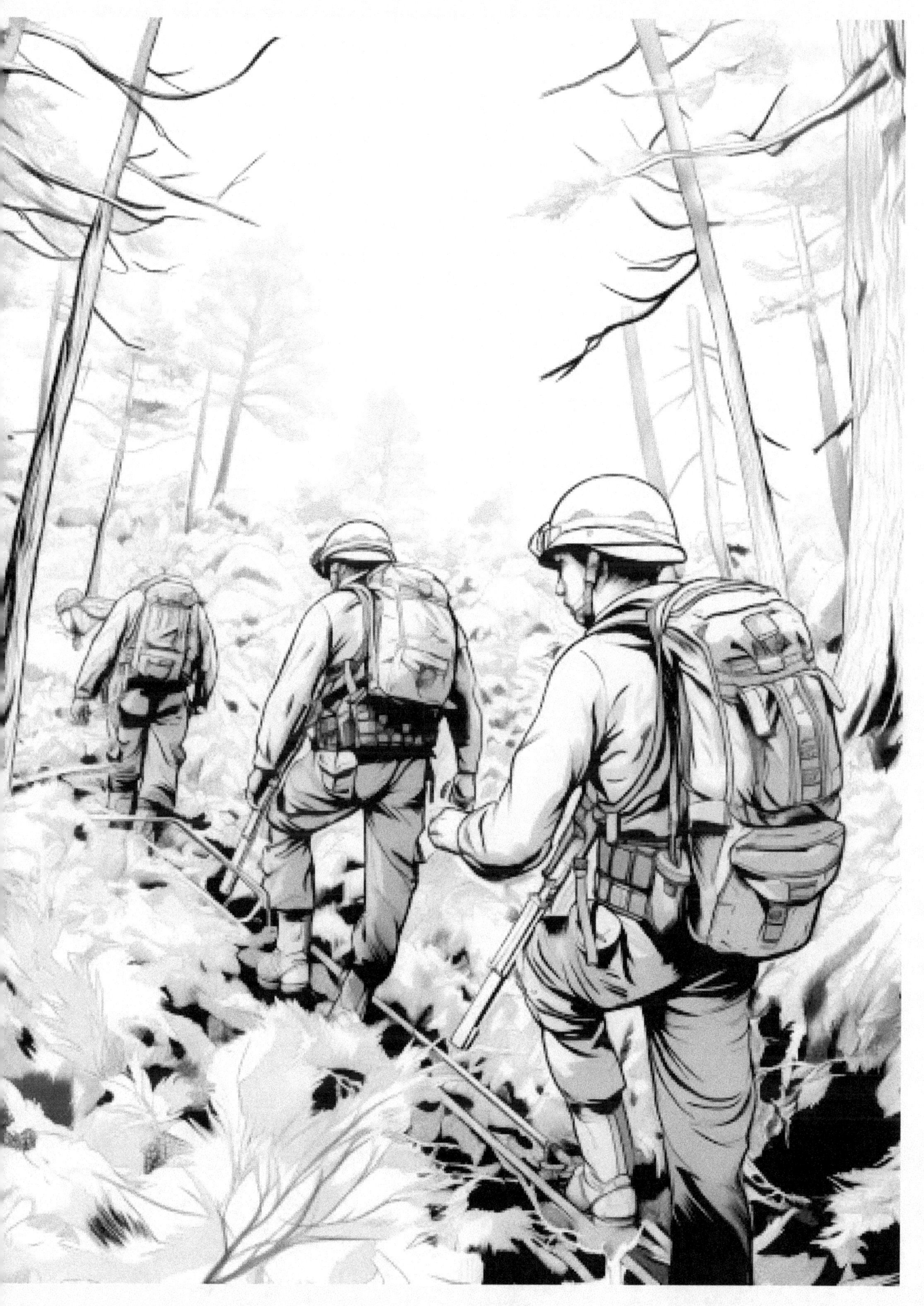

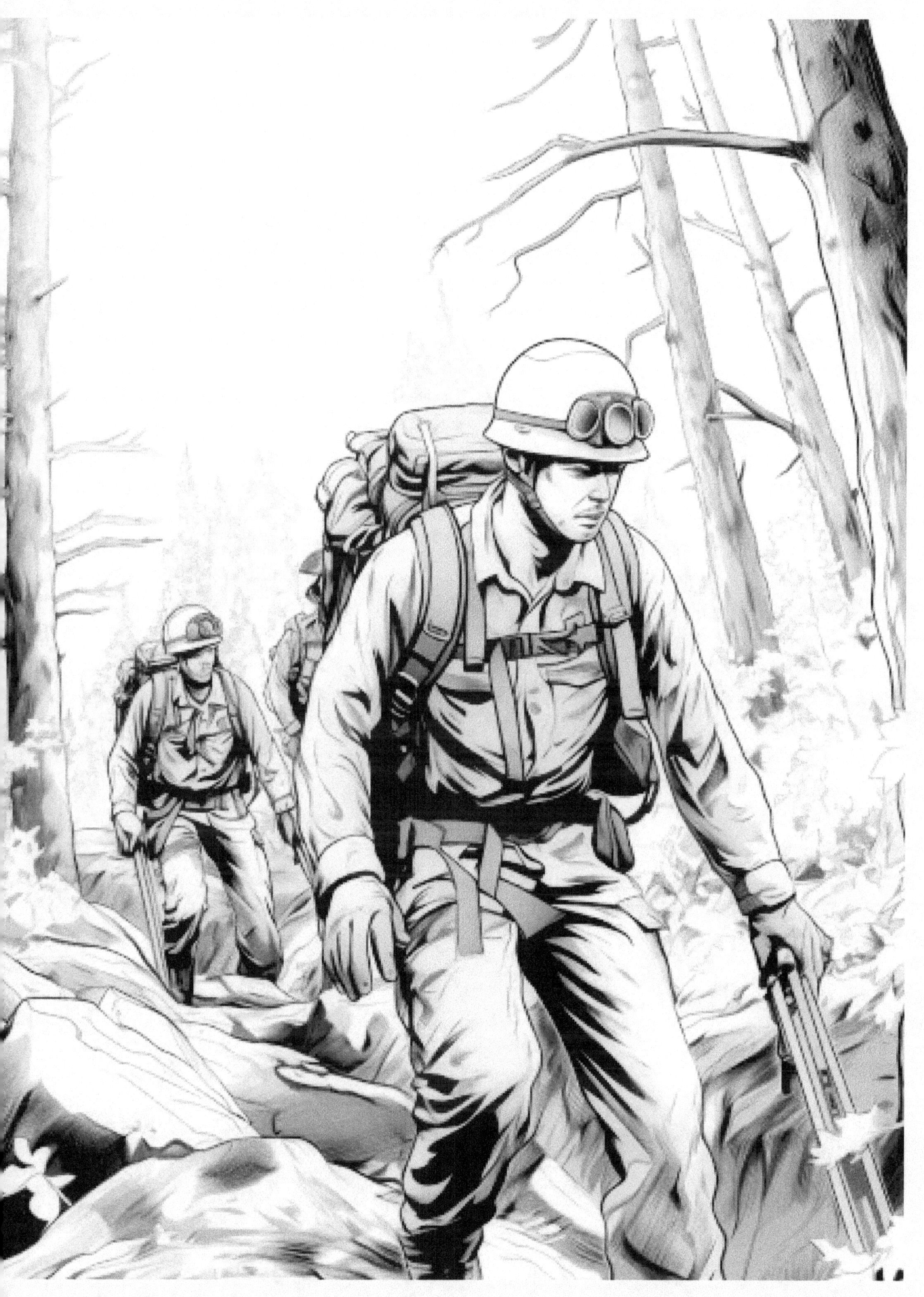

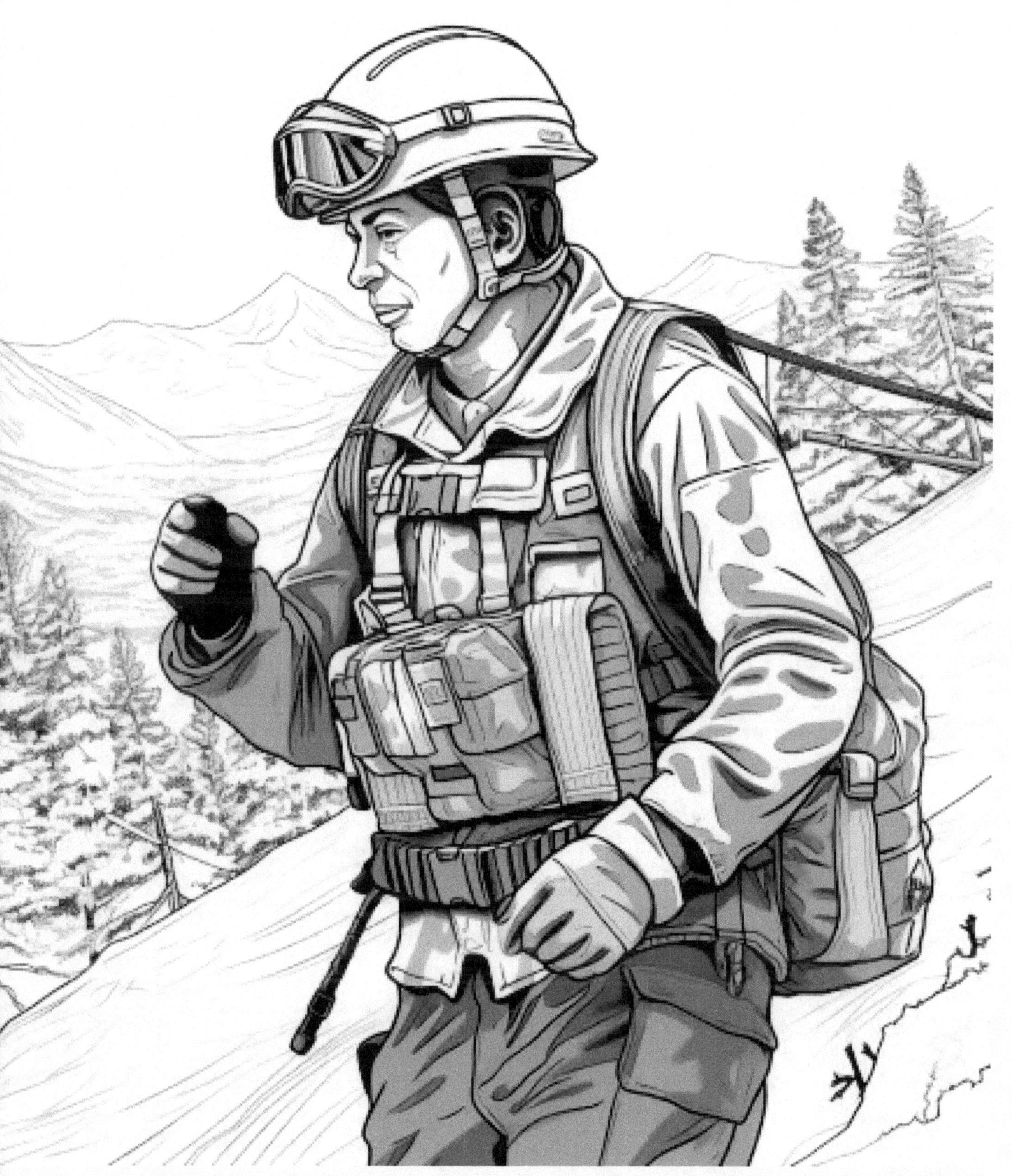

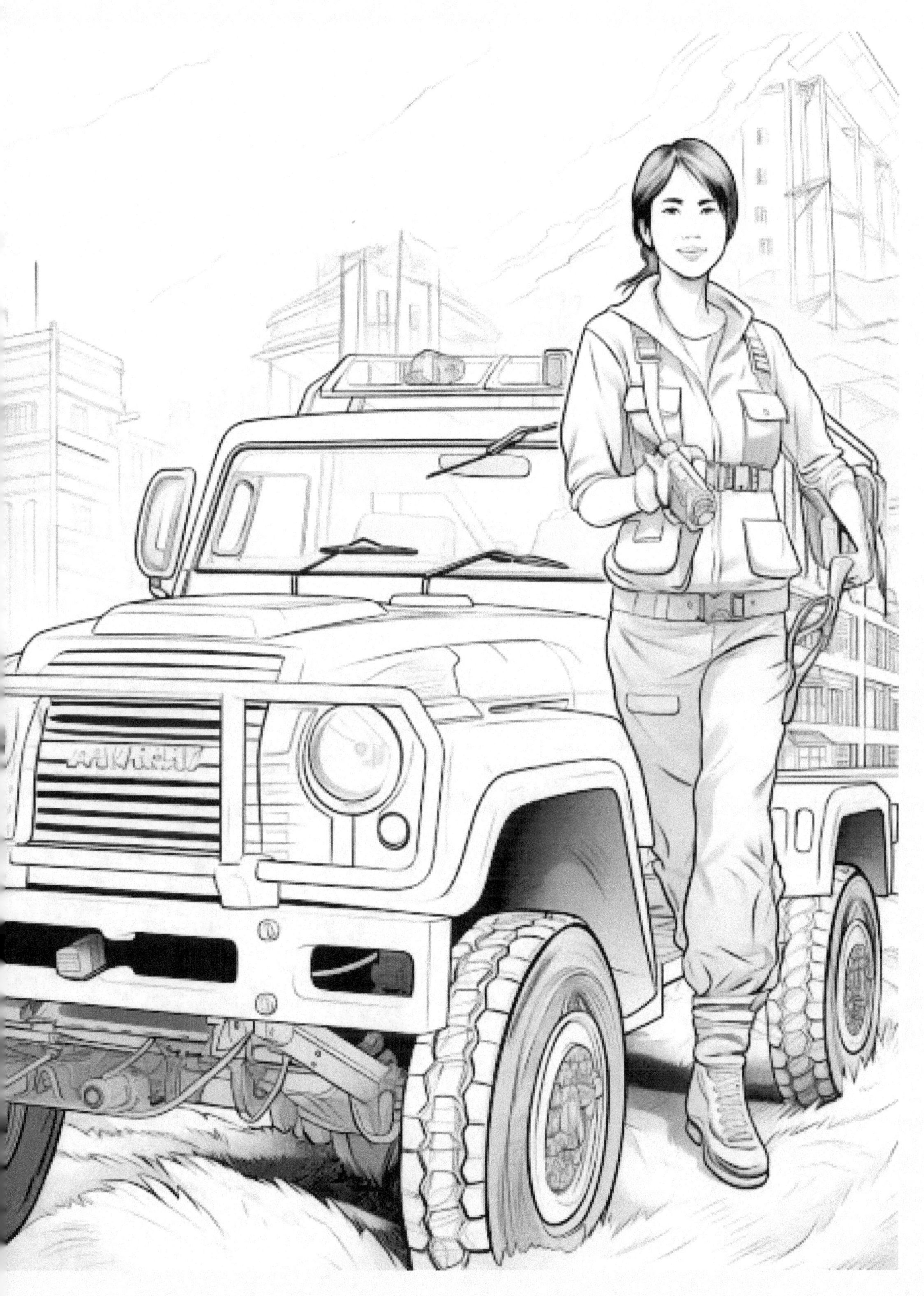

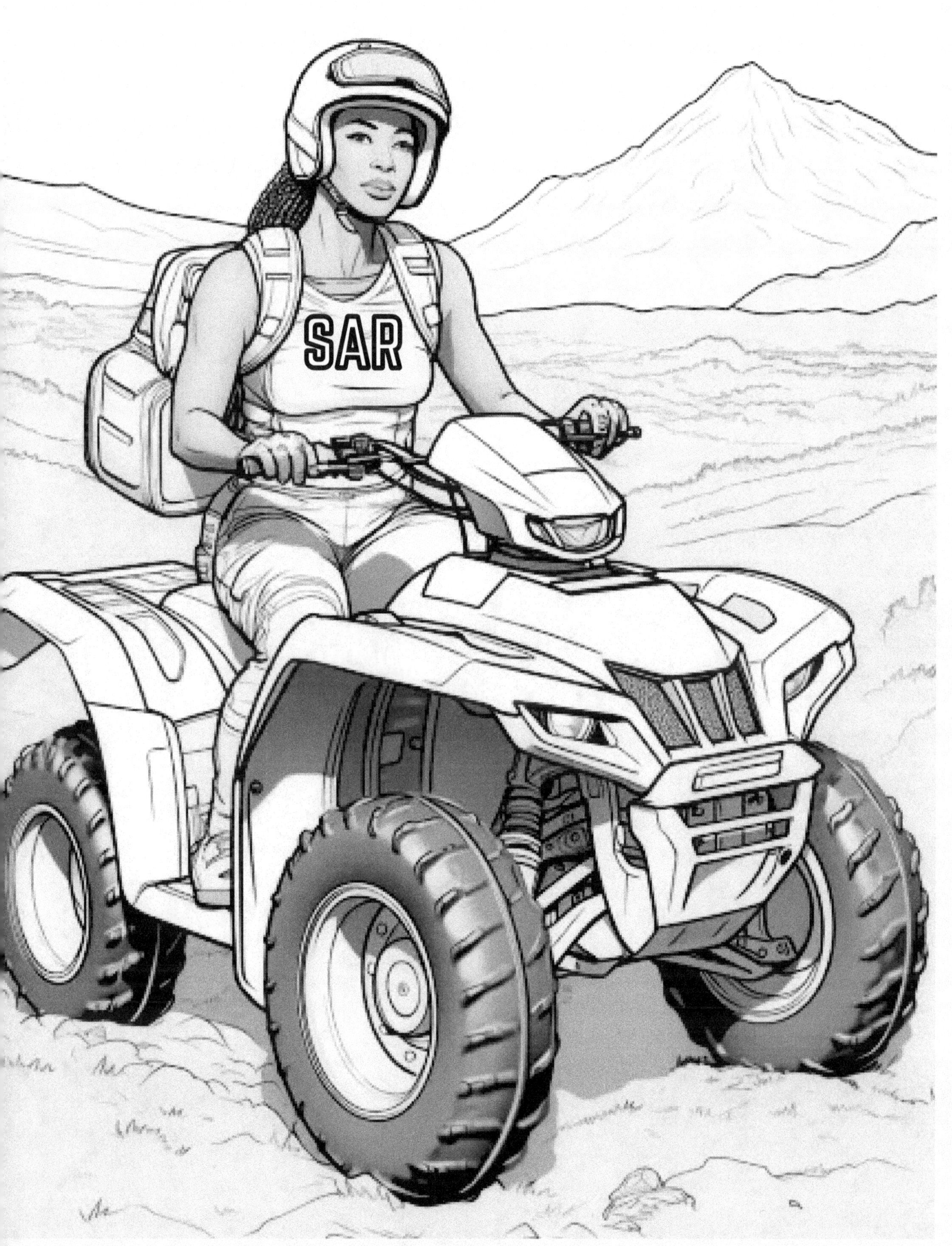
SAR

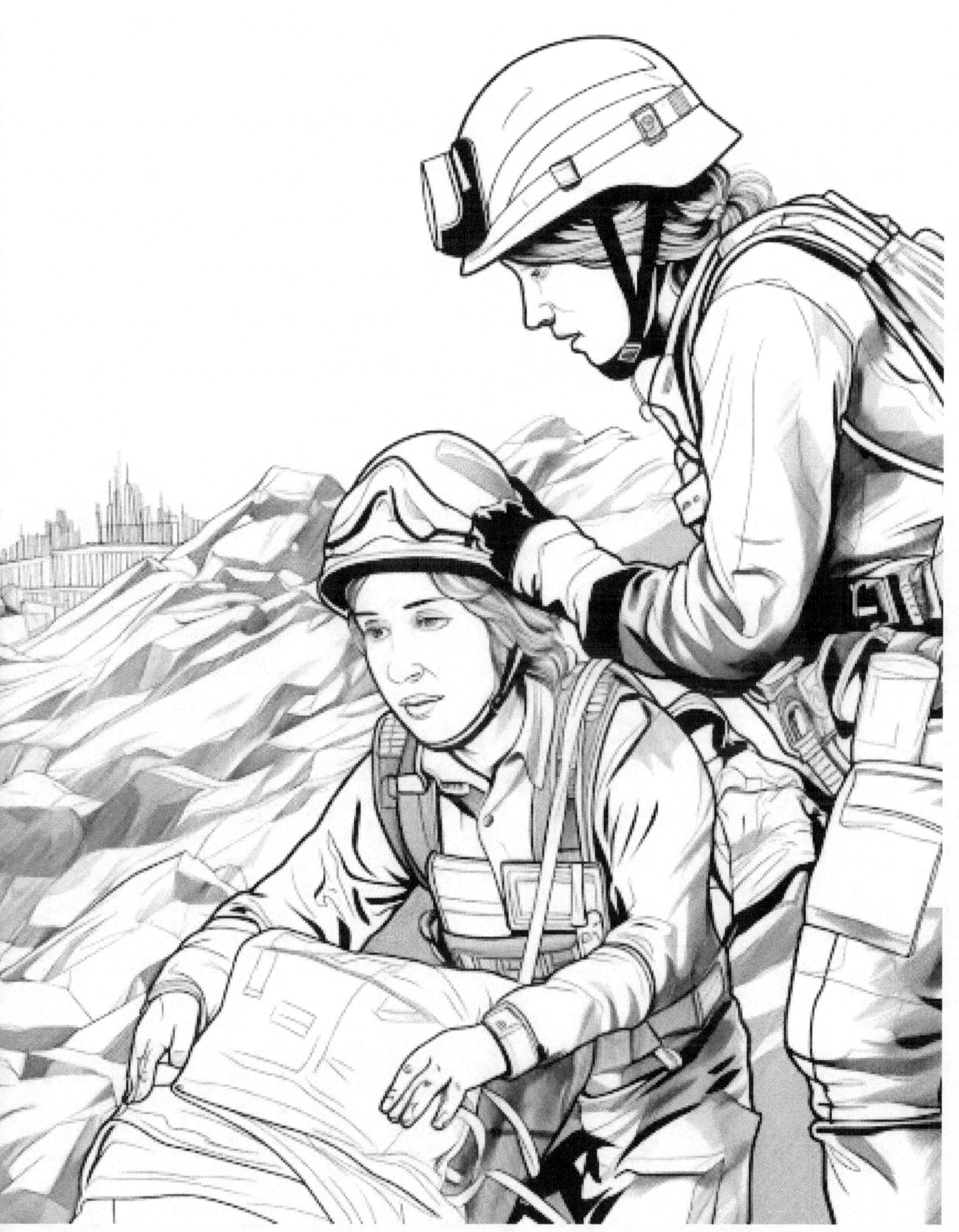

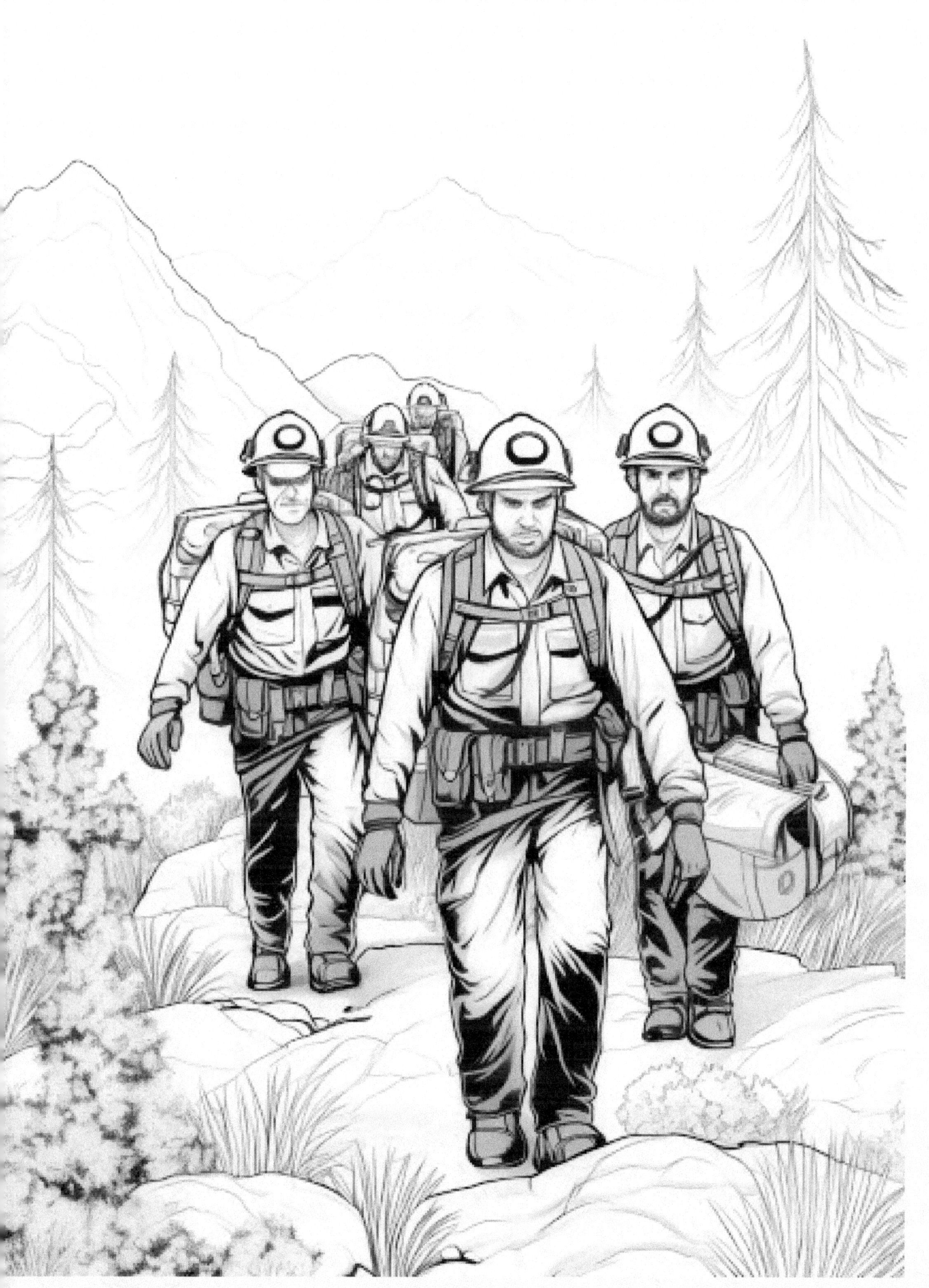

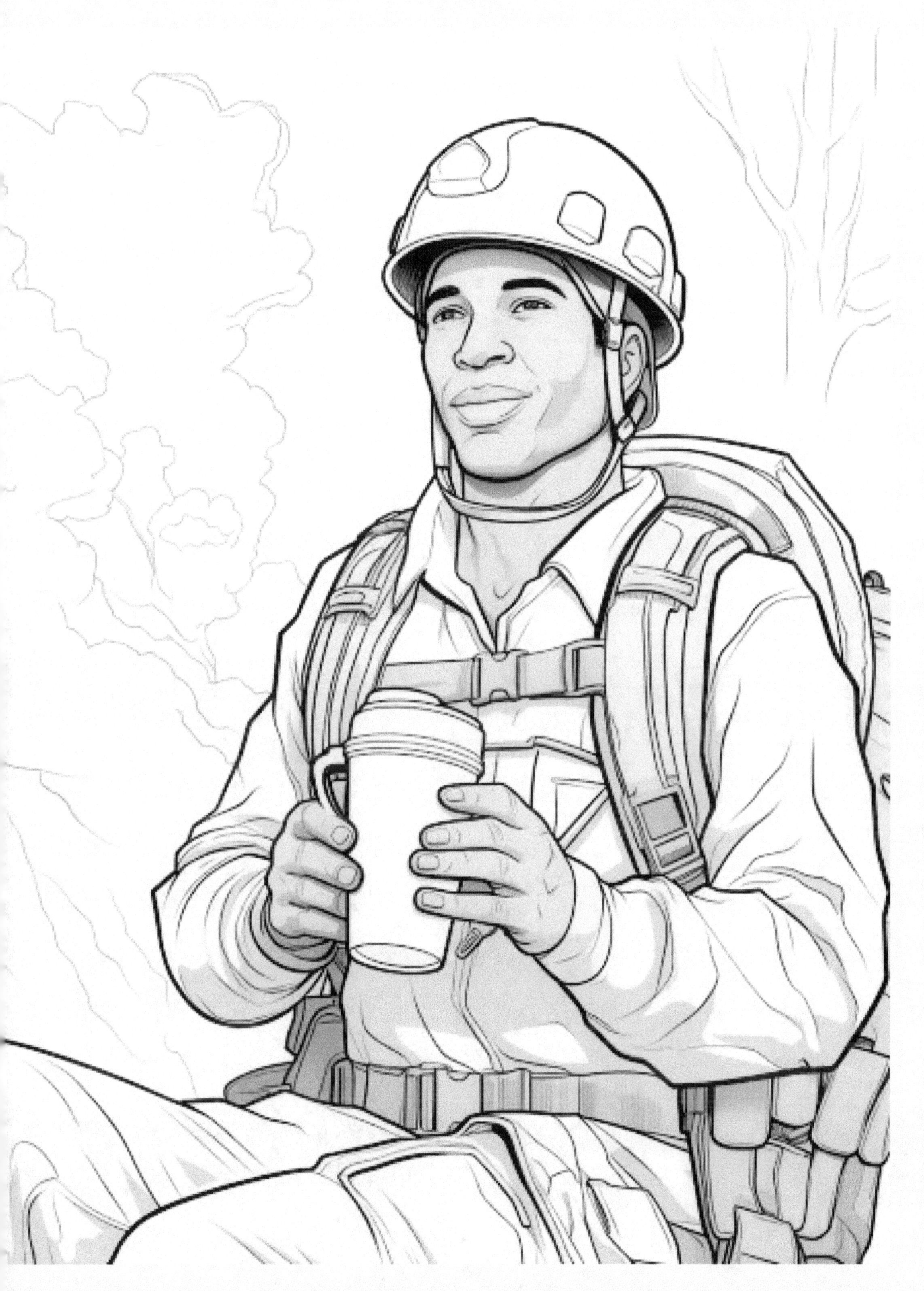

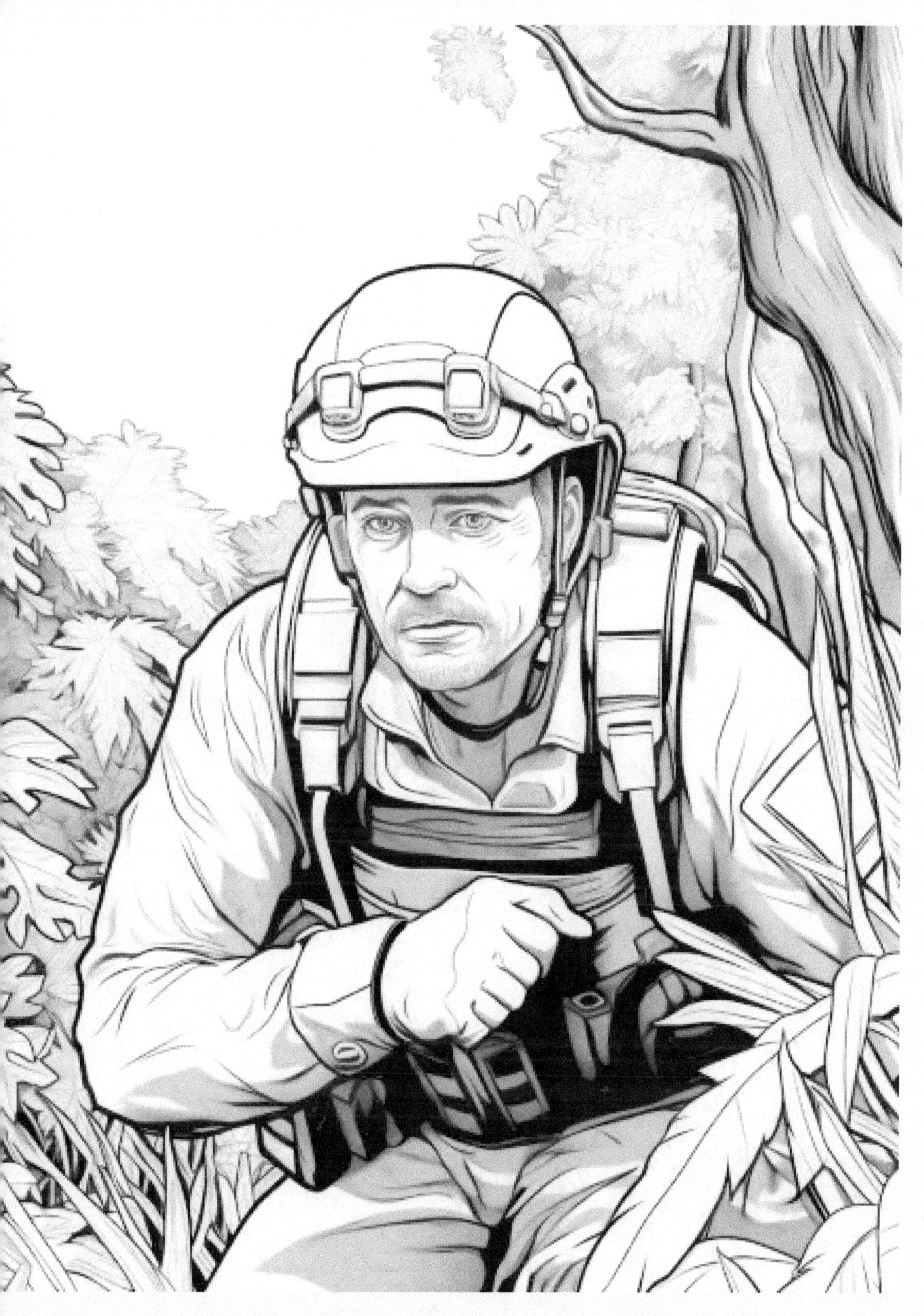

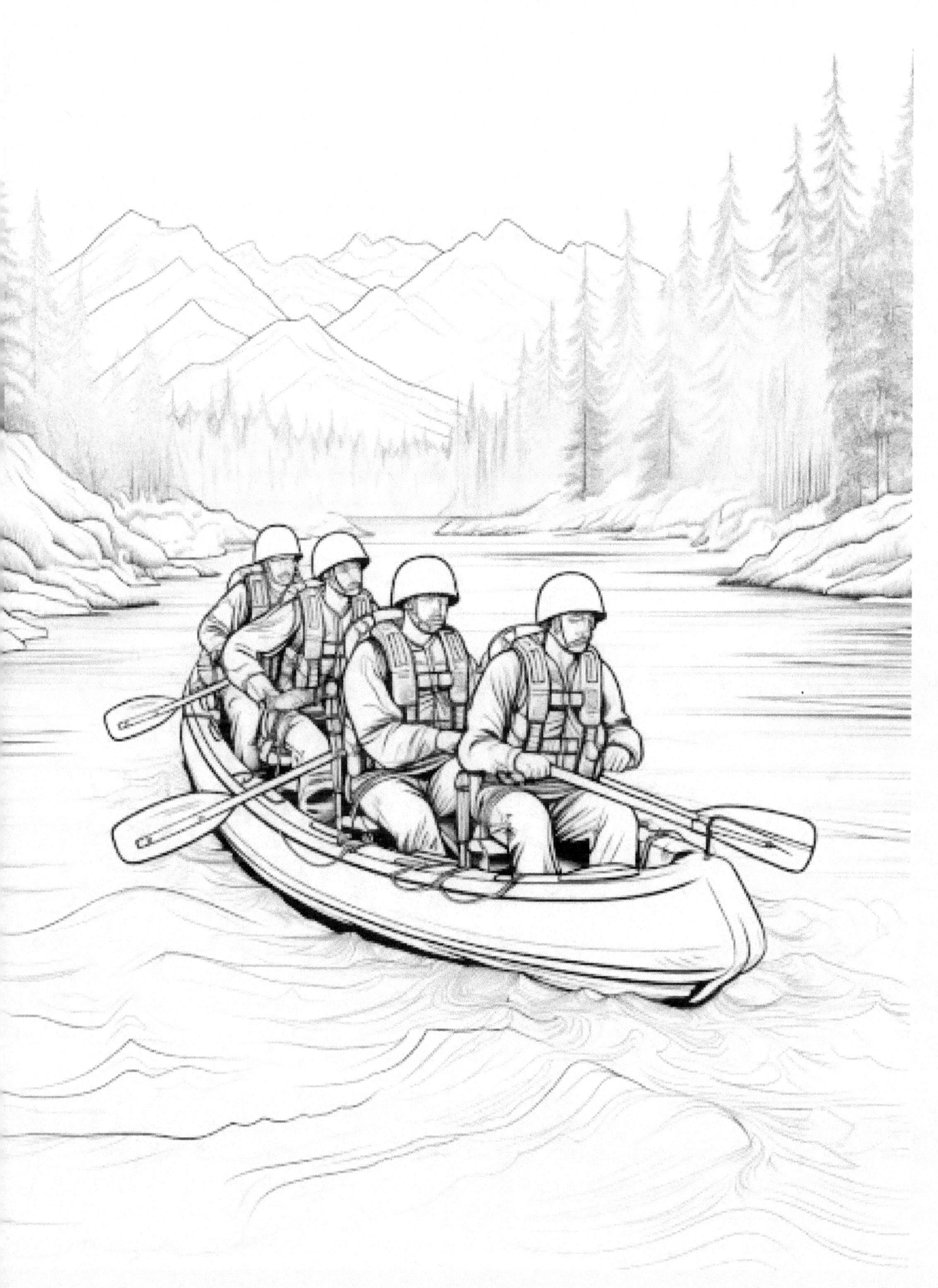

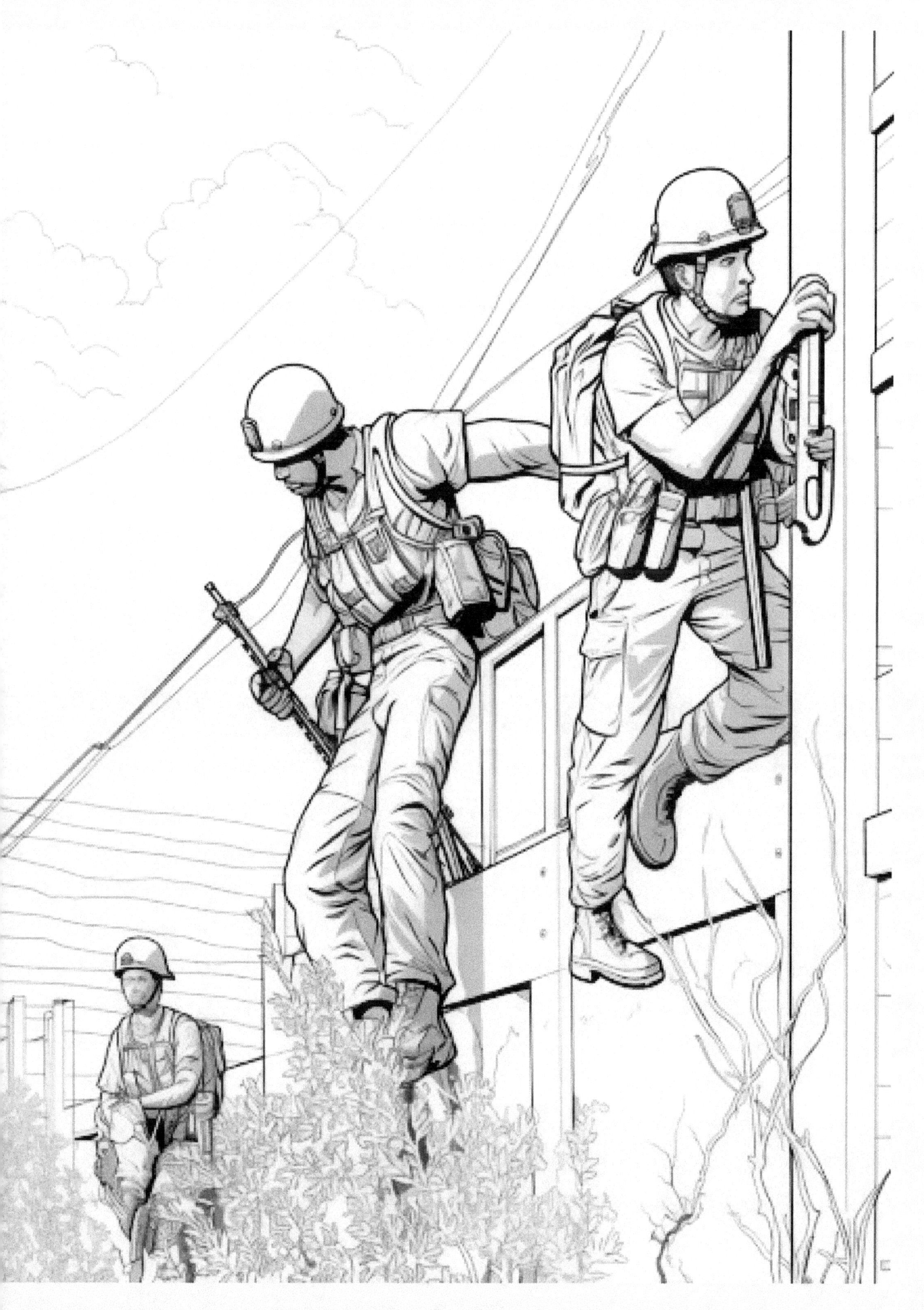

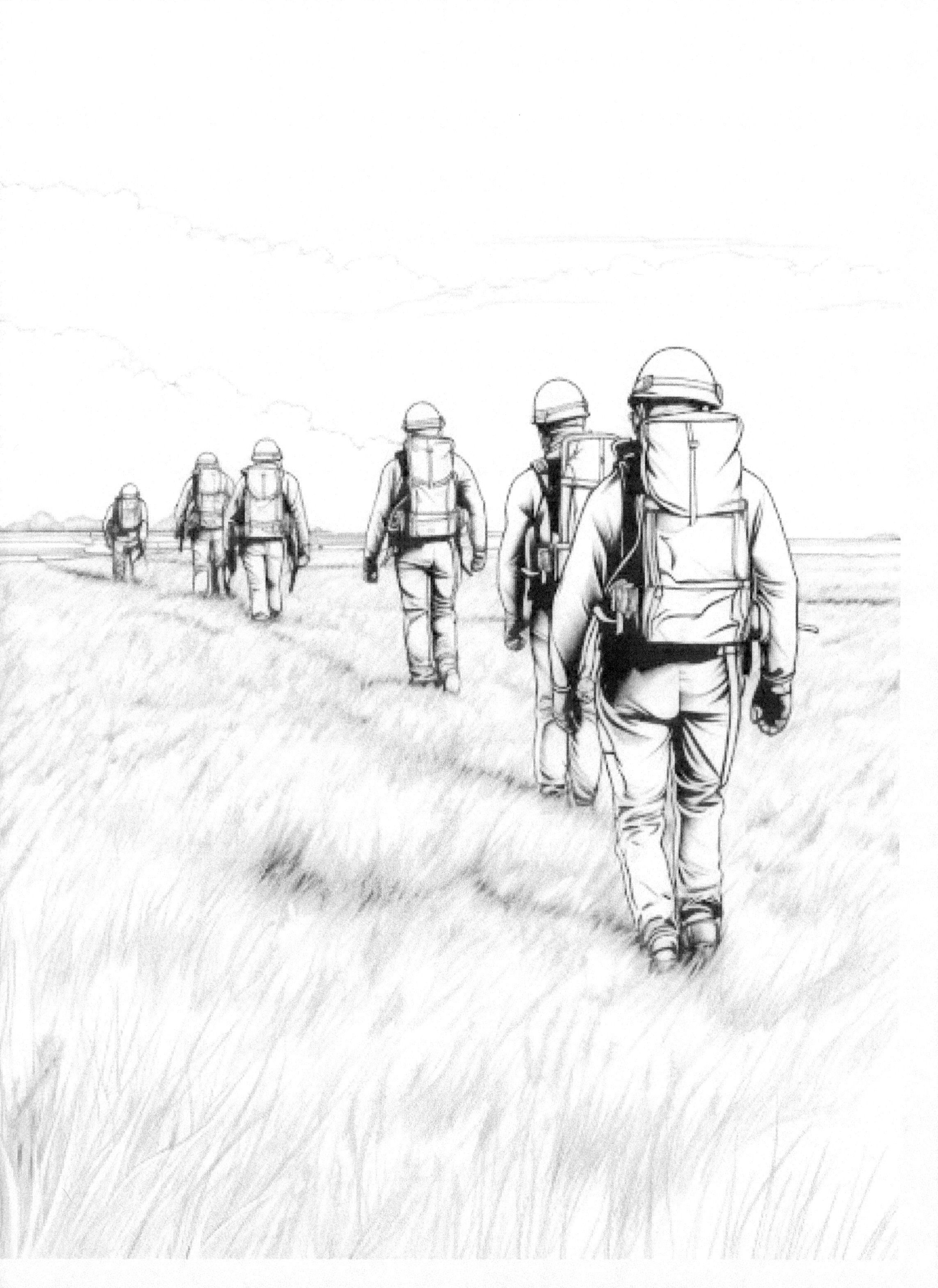

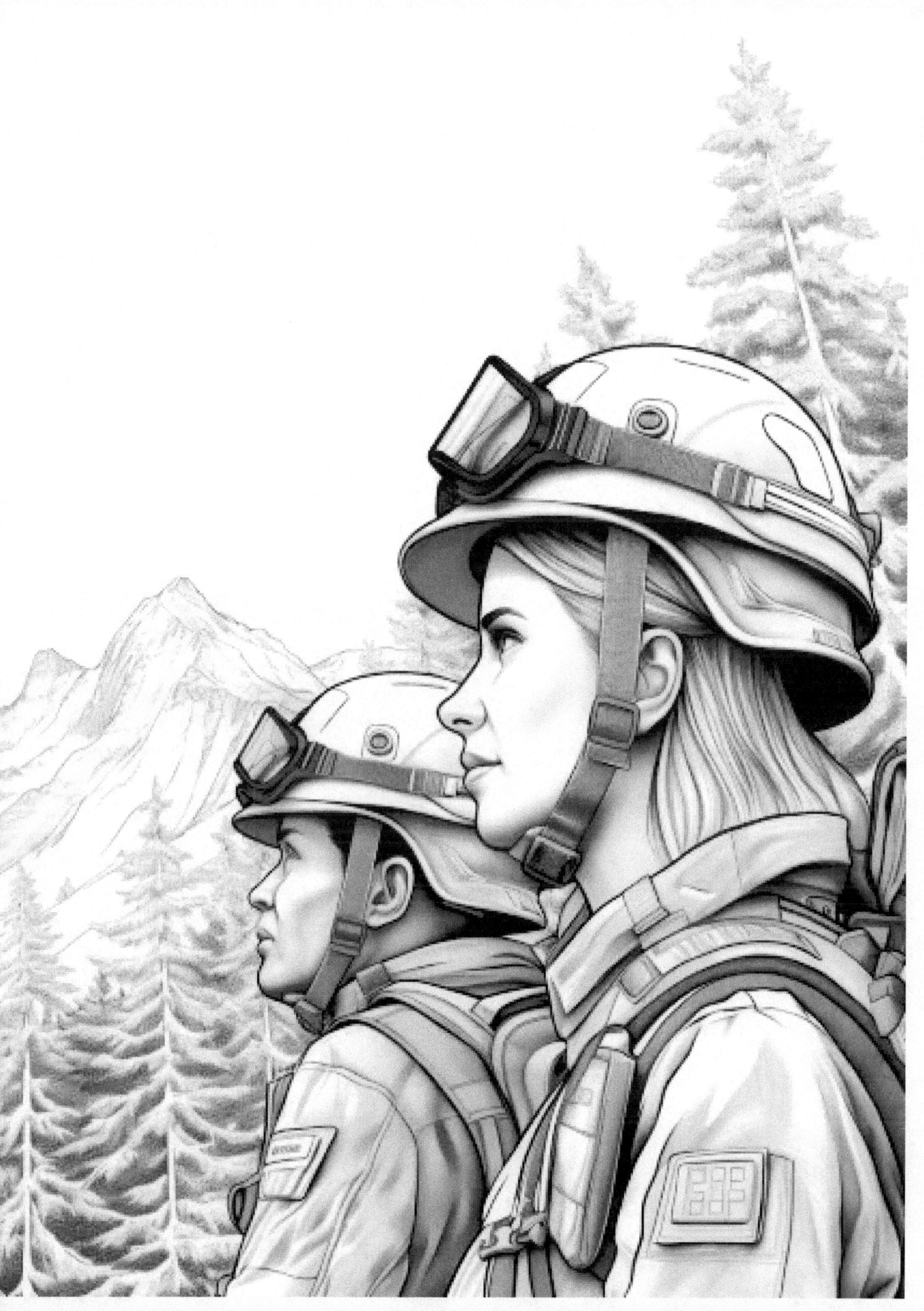

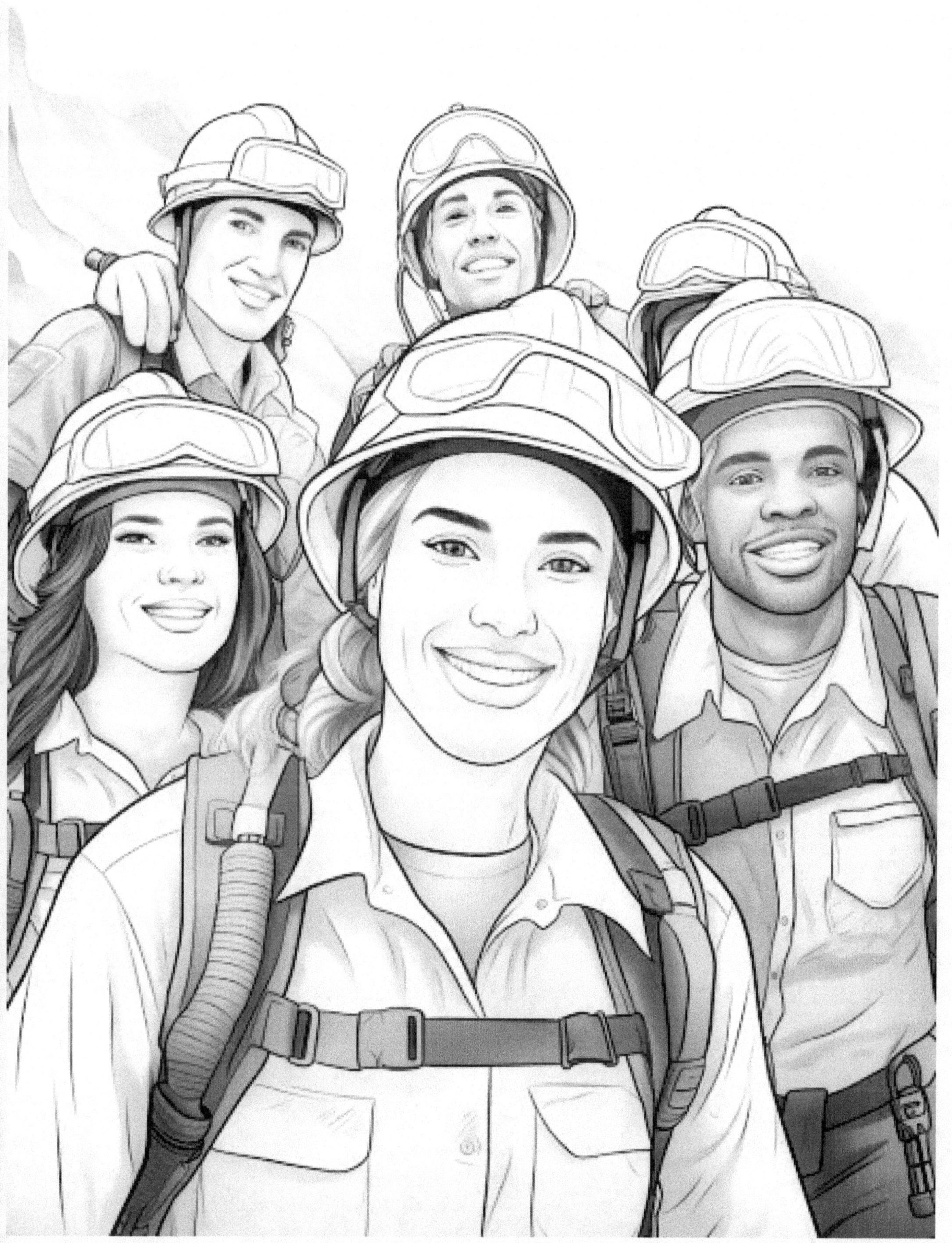